Morality and the Meaning of Life 14

I0112507

MORALITY AND THE MEANING OF LIFE

Edited by:
Professor Albert W.Musschenga (Amsterdam)
Professor Paul J.M. van Tongeren (Nijmegen)

Advisory Board:
Professor Frans De Wachter (Louvain)
Professor Dietmar Mieth (Tübingen)
Professor Kai E. Nielsen (Calgary)
Professor Dewi Z. Phillips (Swansea)

COVENANT AND CONTRACT

Politics, Ethics and Religion

Adela Cortina

PEETERS
LEUVEN - DUDLEY, MA
2003

Library of Congress Cataloging-in-Publication Data

Cortina Orts, Adela.
  Covenant and contract: politics, ethics, and religion / Adela Cortina.
    p. cm. -- (Morality and the meaning of life; 14)
  Includes bibliographical references.
  ISBN 90-429-1340-1
    1. Civil society--Moral and ethical aspects. 2. Social contract--Religious aspects. 3.
Covenants--Political aspects. 4. Political ethics. I. Title. II. Series.

  JC337.C67 2003
  172'.1--dc21

                                                                    2003049843

© Editorial Trotta, S.A., 2001, Madrid
Translated by Andrew Gray for Bolt Traductores e Intérpretes, S.C.

© 2003 — Peeters, Bondgenotenlaan 153, B-3000 Leuven, Belgium
D.2003/0602/93
ISBN 90-429-1340-1

All rights reserved. No part of this publication may be reproduced, stored in a retrieval
system, or transmitted, in any form or by any means, electronic, mechanical, photo-
copying, or otherwise, without the prior permission of the Publisher.

CONTENTS

III. FROM INDIVIDUALISM TO THE POLITICAL COMMUNITY

IV. POLITICAL COMMUNITY AND ETHICAL COMMUNITY

V. CIVIL ETHICS:
BETWEEN THE COVENANT AND THE CONTRACT

VI. THERE IS NO SHADOW WITHOUT A BODY. JUSTICE
AND GRATUITY

At the beginning of the Third Millennium two parables are just as essential as ever to understand human bonds: the Covenant, as told in the book of *Genesis*, and the Contract, which appeared in Hobbes' *Leviathan*. Each of these seems to give meaning to a way of being a person in the modern world, the religious way and the political way, with ethics being left for times of crisis as a substitute for either of these. Nevertheless, politics, ethics and religion continue to be three specific dimensions of the human being, which cannot be properly developed without conveying both the narration of the social contract and that of the covenant from one generation to the next.

In a dialogue with today's most relevant tendencies in thought, this book puts forward a structure of politics, ethics and religion appropriate for our own times, based on the contract between independent beings and the reciprocal recognition of those who are flesh of the same flesh and bone of the same bones.

Prologue

Politics, ethics and religion, whether in this same order, or arranged some other way, are three unrenounceable dimensions of the human being. In the history of the West, and not only here, they have essentially been understood from the standpoint of two accounts, two parables, two stories about human bonds, the one told in the book of *Genesis*, the account of "reciprocal recognition" ("and Adam said: this is now bone of my bones and flesh of my flesh"), and that of Hobbes' *Leviathan*, where the *fiat,* the "let us make man", the creative word uttered by human lips, is the contract by means of which the parts of the body are joined in an artificial political community.

As time has gone by it is the second story that has gradually been absorbing all forms of understanding human bonds, and this dislodgement of the Covenant account has not taken place without a serious loss for the three human dimensions that we are talking about. Democratic politics is deprived of its deepest roots and is turned into weak liberal democracy, ethics becomes a fragile morality by agreement, and religion so often becomes a weapon for use against others or canon law.

In view of the weakening of political virtue a group of thinkers invokes what seems to be a third way of understanding bonds in the city: republicanism, the renaissance of the Aristotelian account, according to which the political community is the home of any other form of relationship, the *res publica* is "prior to" any other form of community. Covenant, Republic and Contract would from this standpoint be the three master formulae for understanding human bonds. Israel, Athens (or the Italian renaissance republics) and London would be their native lands.

Nevertheless, Modernity has not prospered in vain. Republicanism, if it wishes to be modern, turns into liberal republicanism and forgets the community which, according to Aristotle, was such by nature and not by contrivance, opting for commitment to the contract between independent beings as *fiat* of the political world.

But the Contract is not self-sufficient. Anyone who dares to follow the path back to their roots will come to the account of reciprocal recognition. The Covenant is not enough either. Whoever forgets the parable of autonomy will easily disdain justice.

The aspiration of this book is to reveal the mysterious links between the two stories in our political, ethical and religious worlds, and propose that these should continue to be told and above all made material. The text originated in the kind invitation of the Joan Maragall Foundation to give a series of conferences on "Ethics, politics and religion. From individualism to the moral community" in its hall in March 1999. The first version of the lectures was published in Catalan by Cruïlla Publishers. This book is a translation of the revised and extended Spanish version, published in 2001 by Editorial Trotta, Madrid.

I. Two parables on human bonds

1. THE GENESIS AND LEVIATHAN STORIES

1. "It is not good that the man should be alone"

In a fine piece of work entitled "Rebuilding Civil Society: a Biblical Perspective", Great Britain's Chief Rabbi Jonathan Sacks puts forward a thought-provoking thesis[1] for us to ponder over. He asserts that there are two fundamental and fundamentally different ways of thinking of the ties that bind human beings together. One of these forms of thinking is based on the idea of man as a *political animal*, the other on that of man as a *social animal*. And from this difference *two different stories* on the human condition come forth, two accounts which are both true, because they focus on different aspects of life in common, because they are complementary, and in turn give rise to different institutions.

Sacks goes on to show how man, as a *political animal*, creates the institutions proper to political society: States, governments and political systems. As a *social animal*, he creates the institutions proper to civil society: families, communities, voluntary associations and moral traditions. Even though Sacks fails to do so, it is obvious that we must on our own account add at least a further two inescapable domains — the market and public opinion — because without these the field of civil society is actually incomplete. But Sacks avoids these two facets of society in his work, for reasons to be explained further on.

To return to Sacks' article and take this as a connecting theme of the opening to the present work, the relations between political and social institutions, between political society and civil society, were extremely dense in the late 20th and early 21st centuries, but cannot be properly understood without going back to their origin, to the time of creation, as this is told in the book of *Genesis*.

The book of *Genesis* states that in the beginning God made man in his own image and likeness, and thus enjoyed sharing with man the *holiness* that pertained to Him, as God, from that same time. The holiness of the person transmitted by God, that nature of being sacred, inviolable, has since then been one of the characteristics of the person, which the Enlightenment would later translate in a secular version as "absolute value". Man is sacred for man, the person is what is absolutely valuable, and this means that no-one is authorised to treat others or themselves as a means for any ends, that nobody is authorised to exploit human beings, using them only as means for their ends.

---

[1] J. Sacks, "Rebuilding Civil Society: A Biblical Perspective", *The Responsive Community*, vol. 7, n. 1 (1996/97), pp. 11-20.

The wake of man's holiness — the holy, the sacred, the unmanipulable side — has come through human history since then to our own times, to such an extent that Ludwig Feuerbach makes man god for man, "*homo homini deus*". Although this sacred nature of the person for another person is respected very little in everyday life, no-one would dare to reject it verbally because it now belongs to the discourse of what is "ethically correct".[2]

But in the book of *Genesis* Yahweh also openly acknowledges that man is incomplete if he lives as an individual in solitude. Everything was good, and God saw that it was good, but just one shadow was cast on this: man was alone. He needed a fellow-being in whom to recognise himself, as in a mirror, and to be given by this companion a name through which to be really born as a person. This is what entails the *relational* nature of the human being, which reveals the insufficiencies of any selfish egoism. Because in the beginning there was not an isolated individual, and neither was there a community, there was a person in relation to another person.

Nevertheless, this promising beginning —"God saw that it was good"- was soon nipped in the bud, as the book of *Genesis* continues to narrate. Man was holy and existed in relationships, but that very association with another — with woman, in a patriarchal universe- was also the source of unhappiness. The serpent's temptation, Eve's temptation, the fall, the expulsion from Paradise, Cain's fratricide and so on, as far as Yahweh's repentance for having created man and woman, down to the implacable revelation that Noah had: "The end of all flesh is come before me; for the earth is filled with violence through them; and behold, I will destroy them with the earth" (Genesis, 6:13).

How can one form some kind of association, Sacks asks, to make life bearable on earth, after the seed of conflict has germinated? From this question two stories start to be narrated, two very different stories, neither of which should cease to be told. The most modern of these two is recounted in Thomas Hobbes' *Leviathan*, the other being the continuation of the *Old Testament* account.

2. In the beginning was the Contract

In his most famous book, *Leviathan* (1651), Thomas Hobbes recounts the birth of the State, the birth of the *political community*, as arising from a contract between free individuals, with the capacity to sign this. The political community, Hobbes asserts, is not formed naturally, and human beings are not by

---

[2] A. Cortina, *Hasta un pueblo de demonios. Ética pública y sociedad*, Madrid, Taurus, 1998, chap. 3.

4

nature political animals. This is what Aristotle had thought, but he was wrong: the State is *artificially* created by men, and is a monster: the Leviathan, an artificial man, "though of greater stature and strength than the natural man". The soul, which gives life to the whole body, is sovereignty; its artificial joints are magistrates and civil servants; the nerves are reward and punishment, which force the law to be obeyed and thus oblige each member to execute his duty; its power is wealth; its occupation, the people's welfare; counsellors form its memory, while equity and laws are its reason and its will. For the Leviathan illness is sedition, and death is civil war.

But what is the creative act by means of which this artificial man, the State, takes its first breath? The "fiat", Hobbes would say, the "let us make man", the creative word uttered this time by men, not by God, is the *contract* by means of which the parts of the body agree to join.[3] The contract gives life to the political body and maintains this.

It is obviously important here to look into why it is of interest for human beings to sign the contract, as only if the interest is really powerful can one suppose that the parties will keep to what is agreed, and the story of the Leviathan tells us that the reason why men reach the conviction that they should seal the agreement is not magnanimousness nor generosity, but *fear*. In this pessimistic version of human nature, individuals are greedy by nature, each of them wishing to have all the goods of the earth for himself. But as one can suppose that others are similarly rapacious and greedy for goods, one fears losing one's life at others' hands. Anyone, right down to the weakest mortal, can take another's life, and this is what means that man is a predator for man.

Each person's practical reason, which according to Hobbes is *calculating reason*, advises him to seal a non-aggression treaty with others, an agreement by which each renounces his natural greediness to have it all and agrees to join a political community, in which all submit to the law passed by a sovereign. The political community is not formed naturally, but is the product of an artificial contrivance, ultimately based on mutual fear.

In view of the problem posed by the book of *Genesis*, in view of the problem of violence flooding the world through men's malice, the parable of the *Leviathan* says that the most intelligent solution, the one that modern States governed by rule of law have adopted and should fortify, consists in sealing a contract, because men are irremediably selfish individuals, led by a rapacious instinct. Only their fear of losing life and wealth gets under way their reason, which is when all is said and done a calculating reason, and advises them

---

[3] T. Hobbes, *Leviathan. Or the material form and power of a commonwealth, ecclesiastical and civil*, Introduction.

through calculation to sign a self-interested contract with any others who are equally interested for their own sakes, and to form a political community.

Obviously, Hobbes does not think that this process actually takes place. Signing the contract is not a historical fact that occurred in a particular place at a particular time. The story of the Leviathan does not attempt to reply to the question about origins — "how did political order start?", but to the question about sufficient reason — "why should I obey laws and governors?". This is a metaphor, a parable, a way of understanding why men agree to live in a political community and to submit to the power of law. They do so because this is selfishly of interest to them, for their own sakes.

We should like to point out here that the contract is curiously primarily an instrument of private law, particularly appropriate for organising the mercantile world under the logic of give and take. I sign a contract with those who can give me something in exchange, not with those who have very little or nothing to offer. Mercantilisation comes into political life in the form of the contract, when it is understood that the community has its roots in a self-seeking interest agreement, by means of which all undertake to let themselves be governed by law.

Nevertheless, as soon as we recognise that the driving force behind political life is self-interest, conflicts prove to be inevitable and the following step is to establish a power that would make the law complied with by coercion. The *keys* to political life are thus *selfish individualism, calculating reason, the self-interested contract, the mercantilisation of shared life, latent conflict* and *coercion:* keys that do not seem the least unfamiliar in the political life of the early 21st century.

Is this really the only way to establish bonds between humans beings so as to prevent violence from flooding the earth, whether this is what was experienced by the author of Chapter 6 of *Genesis*, or as undergone by Hobbes in mid-17th century England? Is there no other way of binding these beings — humans — who say they are and wish to be free, at the same time as preventing conflicts from destroying the face of the earth?

3. In the beginning was the Covenant

To return to Jonathan Sacks' work, The *Old Testament* gives us a different view of human ties: the version of the *covenant*, as opposed to that of the *contract*[4].

---

[4] Indeed, the term "covenant" is used in the Bible to refer to the relationship between God and man, and the different biblical traditions endow the term with different shares of meaning. The first time the covenant appears, after the Flood, its meaning is that of a promise, a bond which nothing can dissolve (*Genesis*, 9: 8-17). In this book we take the term "covenant" in this sense of a bond which nothing can annul to refer to the way Adam sees the bond linking him with Eve:

For when Yahweh discovers that man's solitude is bad, he does not suggest that he should seal an agreement. Instead he gives him a companion, and he *recognises* her as part of himself, as "flesh of his flesh and bone of his bones". This is the account, not of the contract, but of *mutual recognition*, the narration, not of the agreement, but of the *covenant* between those who become aware of their human identity. Until that time man was known by the name "*adam*", which means "man as part of nature", but after Eva's recognition, this becomes "ish", "man as a person"

This thus opens up the approach of a dialogical personalism,[5] because the human being has to pronounce the name of another human being before knowing his own name, and has to say "you" before he can say "I", recognising his own *identity* through the relationship with another at least partly identical to himself.[6]

From this basic recognition of each other the driving force behind social relations cannot be self-interest, but *compassion*, though not understood as condescension with an inferior in an asymmetric relationship, but as "enduring with" others the suffering and happiness which are felt when realising that one is part of them.

This leads to a type of *obligations* which are not the stipulations of a contract before a notary. Whoever signs a contract can free oneself from it as soon as it ceases to interest them and is possible to do so, a case which tends to arise precisely in difficult times; while someone who recognises the other as a part of themselves and is aware of being bound to them by a covenant does not break the bond in difficult times, but instead defends it with greatest might precisely in these times.

It could be said, to go on with the differences between these two types of bonds, that the contract, when not of interest, is maintained by *external power*, by coercion, whilst the covenant is maintained by means of a personally assumed *internalised sense* of *identity*, *loyalty*, *obligation* and *reciprocity*.

The contract, Sacks would add, is the basis for political society and gives rise to the instruments of the State (governments, political systems), the covenant being the basis for civil society and leading to families, communities and voluntary associations.

---

there is a ligature and thus an ob-ligation between them. Adam and Eve do not seal an agreement of convenience; they recognise instead the bond already existing.

[5] In Spain personalism has a great debt to such renowned philosophers as Carlos Díaz, who has not only developed this in his own publications (some of which are *Contra Prometeo*, Madrid, Encuentro, 1980; *Corriente Arriba*, Madrid, Encuentro, 1985; *De la razón dialógica a la razón profética*, Móstoles, Madre Tierra, 1991, *La política como justicia y pudor*, Móstoles, Madre Tierra, 1992, or *Soy amado, luego existo. Yo y tú*, Bilbao, Desclée de Brouwer, 1999), but also has given rise to the magazine *Acontecimiento* and to the *Esprit* collection, directed by A. Simón at Caparrós Editores. Also, in this sense, see A. Domingo *Un humanismo del siglo XX: el personalismo* (Madrid, Cincel, 1985); A. Simón, *La experiencia de alteridad en la fenomenología trascendental*, Madrid, Esprit, 2001.

[6] M. Buber, *Ich und Du*, 1923.

So far we have taken Sacks' work as a connecting theme and will continue to do so in a further two affirmations, to then go on to state our discrepancies and put forward a hypothesis.

The *first* of these assertions, with which I totally agree, is that these two stories on the bonds which connect human beings and which can prevent violence and war are *true and complementary*. It is not a matter of refuting one of them and being left with a single narration, because both of them have their own part of truth, which is why *both have to be told*. And this is a statement which in my opinion one should keep hold of and apply to everyday life. There are a number of stories on the life of human beings which one should continue to tell, which cannot be silenced, which must "be available" for all those who can receive them and recognise themselves in them.

And nevertheless, — this is the second assertion I should like to reaffirm — *in the last two centuries the two stories that we have been using have not been told to the same extent.* The parable of the covenant has been relegated to a second plane, until practically falling into oblivion, while the parable of the contract has been used not only to interpret how the State is formed and how the market operates, but also to interpret social institutions as a whole. The discourse of the contract, rights, interest groups, factions and parties, has not only been used in the past and is still being used in the political world, but has also seeped into social life and has conquered this, so that families and civil associations increasingly understand each other in terms of contracts, rights and duties.

As regards religion, it is important to dissolve with Sacks such a widely-extended platitude as the one asserting that it has been modern science which has undermined the foundations of theology through considering only what can be measured and proven true or false as rational. Since, as has been said time and time again, modern science prepares hypotheses whose consequences have to be submitted to quantification and falsation, anything that goes beyond these parameters is relegated, so that the world lost all its bonds with mystery. The modern rationalisation process, as has also been affirmed ad nauseam, went along with a process of "disenchantment", because the realm of magic cannot come within the coordinates of what can be verified or proved false.

Sacks nevertheless affirms, and quite rightly too, that it is not the scientific and technical form of thought that gradually pushed aside the religious story of Judean and Christian tradition, but *the imperialism of the political and economic form of thinking*. He categorically states that "the real drama of the last century was not religion being eclipsed by science, but religious forms of thinking about human relations being eclipsed by political and economic models ".[7]

---

[7] J. Sacks, "Rebuilding Civil Society: A Biblical Perspective", p. 17.

Nevertheless, he goes on, without civil society, without trust, even political and economic structures fail, which is why it is important to restore the great narrative which sees our social relations in terms of covenant and reciprocity. This is why it is important to go on telling the two stories, but particularly that of the covenant, which is the one that has gradually been left unuttered for the last two centuries. Is all this true?

2. THREE UNRENOUNCEABLE FORMS OF BEING A PERSON

1. Not only the capacity to contract

There is doubtlessly a great deal of truth in the work that we took as a connecting theme in the previous chapter, but to retrieve this one should remember the context in which it was written, for what purpose, and what items are to be taken from it in this book, which will obviously have its own direction.

Firstly, the quarterly journal, *The Responsive Community. Rights and Responsibilities*, in which the article appears, has been published in the United States since January 1991 as an express platform for the communitarian movement.[8] Current communitarianism, one should remember, is a movement born in the nineteen-eighties as a reaction to a supposed liberal imperialism. Communitarians understand that in both political life and in the economy and ethics liberal ideology has taken over and done away with any other way of thinking. Although liberalism comes forward as a tolerant ideology, communitarians nevertheless affirm that this is in fact gradually taking over all spheres of social life and forcing out any other form of political, economic and social proposal as if this were irrational. What liberalism actually does is to identify "rationality" with "liberal rationality" in all fields, and reject what does not abide by its canons as being irrational. Rawls' very proposal of reinforcing a reasonable pluralism starts from the conviction that what is reasonable is restricted to the moral core of liberalism.

This led some authors to taking a stand against liberal imperialism in the nineteen-eighties, still without proposing any genuine alternative model, but simply subjecting this to intense criticism.[9] Nevertheless, the communitarian movement began to propose real alternatives to the liberal model in the nineties

---

[8] On this point see the introduction by À. Castiñeira to *Communitat i nació*, Barcelona, Proa, 1995, pp. 9-26.

[9] This is the case of A. MacIntyre (*After Virtue*, London, Duckworth, 1981), M. Sandel (*Liberalism and the Limits of Justice*, Cambridge University Press, 1982) or M. Walzer, ("The communitarian critique of liberalism", in *Political Theory*, vol. 18, n° 1 (1990), pp. 6-23).

and, apart from the usual publications, the main means of expression is the magazine *The Responsive Community*.[10]

Although the communitarian movement is characterised, amongst other aspects, by the heterogeneity of its members, one of the facets common to almost all of them is the desire to promote civil society. As opposed to the State monopoly, which in the Eastern countries destroyed civil society and in liberal countries ends up absorbing other social spheres through the way it behaves, communitarians and thinkers backing this movement stress the importance of civil society.[11] This is why the article "Rebuilding Civil Society" attempts *to compare two ways of understanding human bonds (contract and covenant)* by assigning one of these to man as a *political animal*, but as a *political animal within the liberal politics prevailing in everyday life*, and the other to man as an *animal of civil society*, but excluding *market relations and sectors such as that of public opinion from civil society*. The reader thus immediately and schematically understands that the society based on the covenant must be strengthened, not allowing it to perish under contractual individualism.

Sacks himself has developed this schematic view at greater length in a book which has the beautiful title of *The Politics of Hope*,[12] and in which he goes as far as apocalyptical statements about liberal societies with which I do not agree in the least, apart from rejecting the simplistic "social division" of work propounded, by which politics is associated with contract, and civil society with covenant. Social reality, fortunately or unfortunately, is always more complex.

This is why such a thought-provoking interpretation as the one given in "Rebuilding Civil Society" should lead us to take note of what is undeniably true in this, but also to point out what is not so acceptable and propose new possibilities.

As far as *agreement* is concerned we must first stress one basic concurrence: it proves difficult to deny that in the liberal political discourse on rights, duties, the contract, factions and interest groups have "colonised" the other discourses of social life, and that the relations between people are increasingly understood on all levels as relations of reciprocal rights and duties.

In the family, in the groups traditionally considered as being "primary solidarity" groups, at schools, hospitals, religious institutions, universities, in any social sphere, the different members of these interpret their relations more and more in terms of rights, duties, agreements and interest groups. This is not only

---

[10] As regards these publications, see in particular the works by A. Etzioni, editor of the magazine *The Responsive Community*, *The New Golden Rule*, New York, Basic Books, 1996; *The limits of privacy*, New York, Basic Books, 1999.

[11] M. Walzer, "The Civil Society Argument", in Ronald Beiner (ed.), *Theorizing Citizenship*, State of New York Press, 1995, pp. 153-174.

[12] J. Sacks, *The Politics of Hope*, Jonathan Cape, 1997.

a matter of their having to abide by the legal framework, as is proper to any form of association encountered in the sphere of a political community configured as a Constitutional State, but of the internal relations of the members of the association being understood on these terms.

People then start to talk about "democratic families" simply to indicate that these are families in which there is no ill-treatment, in which each of the members is taken into account, without perceiving that the *humus* of family life should be mutual affection, tenderness, constant concern, all of these "*obligations*" (it is an important term to coin) which in spite of the efforts of north American judges and psychologists, cannot be demanded by law. There is no reason why families and groups of friends should aspire to become institutions which work by the "one man, one vote" system, but should aspire to something else.

This should also be the case with institutions in civil society, such as universities, whose aim should really consist in forming the *êthos*, the character of those who aspire to truth and to good in a de-prejudiced community. Reducing the university to the game of politics, whether played by professional politicians or the usual amateurs, can only lead to corrupting this, i.e., to perverting what should be its own nature.

It is obviously necessary for the different civil associations to abide by law in force to prevent abuse, humiliations and exploitation. No member of a civil association is legitimated to violate the rights of others, by alleging that in this sphere not only rights have to be respected, but what matters above all is to live from affection, compassion or the community bond. This terrible excuse has been used excessively to justify ill-treatment, deceit and abuse, and this is why it is important for the members of the different civil associations to be able to be legally defended. But it is none the less true that the nature of the bonds between these associations' members is perverted when it is *only* understood in terms of duties and rights, demands, contracts, agreements and factions; when the relationship is conceived in these terms to such an extent that we cut ourselves off from the possibility of thinking and living any other form of relationship, based not so much on mutual demands as on the covenant, not so much on rights and duties undertaken as on the fullness of the heart.

Doubtlessly the duty not to harm anyone ("*neminem laede*") is an ancient social conquest stated at the beginning of modern codes of law, but it dates back at least to Roman law and is recognised worldwide even as the first of the principles of Bioethics, that of non-maleficence. In the family, in the neighbourhood, in the churches and other religious institutions, or in the relationships between people from different countries, no-one has the right to harm others. But forming this background mentality, according to which no-one is *bonded to others* if this is not by contractual ties of rights and duties, is an infallible way to dry up the wellsprings of shared life, an implacable way to

11

erase the enjoyment of mutual relations little by little. For the bonds between human beings are precisely happiness-creating when their permanence is not demanded by coercion, not even by voluntarily accepted coercion.

And apart from this, drying up the sources, pulling up the roots, also ends up leading to depriving of meaning even the discourse of rights (which is, as we shall see, not self-sufficient). One of the essential aims of this book consists precisely in *showing how, to have any meaning, the discourse of the contract and rights needs the presupposition of the account of the covenant and of the obligations born from reciprocal recognition.* If that account and that obligation fade away, it will gradually be seen that the usual method of proclaiming over and over again the importance of human rights, in a reiterative procedure which consists, as Juan Antonio Ortega pointed out, in insisting with the deceased Amália Rodrigues that "é uma casa portuguesa com certeza, é com certeza uma casa portuguesa" — has limits which cannot be passed. The generations whom nobody told about the account of the roots, the sources, end up asking "why?" without getting any answer. Living without answers is not a good thing for human beings, who end up discarding what they learned only by wearisome insistence.

It is obvious that the question "why should I respect human rights?" could be answered "because, ultimately, it is of interest to you, because your rights will be better protected in a society in which everyone respects each other than in one in which they do not". And this type of answer is one that gets under way the whole world of theories of rational decision, in which the aim is to generate "virtuous circles" as opposed to "vicious circles": those who enjoy the advantages of mutual respect will reinforce good habits of respect, and in such a society cooperating will prove to be reasonable. On the other hand, where people are ill-treated, respecting others can almost be irrational, and therefore individuals reinforce their conduct of not respecting each other, thus generating a vicious circle, diametrically opposed to the previous one, which was a virtuous circle. It is important to *induce* people to respect each other, more than to persuade them to *recognise each other* as being respectable.

Nevertheless, virtuous circles thus generated have many limits, and not only because there are inevitably stowaways, those who enjoy a voyage without paying their fare, without complying with the law, but because modern political life has requirements which far exceed the capacity to contract, and demand recognition. Human practical reason is not only strategic rationality, able to calculate what is advantageous for those who make use of it, but much more than this.

However, going back to the account of the covenant, it is true that this has been left in the background. There are clearly people who continue to *live* from this, in both the religious sphere and in non-religious solidarity associations (*SOs*, rather than *NGOs*), in which people who "do not keep account of the good that they do" work. But it is true that the account is told less and less all

12

the time, and nevertheless one should do so because it is not good for attitudes to lose their roots, as we shall see further on. This is why this book will take the capacity to contract and the capacity to enter into the covenant as two forms of interpreting human bonds, two non-eliminable forms in human co-existence, and recognise with Sacks that the discourse of the contract has gone far beyond the sphere in which it has any legitimacy and has colonised that of the covenant, sending this into exile.

2. Political animal, social animal

However, at least *three things* prove rather open to question, the first two referring to "man as a political animal" and the second to "man as a social animal". As far as "man as a political animal" is concerned, it is not true either that people's political capacity can be identified merely with the capacity for contracting, nor that the contract by means of which the political community is created can only be interpreted from the standpoint of the Leviathan. As far as "man as a social animal" is concerned, neither is it true that the relations which bind people in civil society are only covenant relations, and are not also contract and transgression relations. These three rectifications are not in the least anodyne, as they radically disrupt Sacks' simple viewpoint, which identifies politics with contract, and civil society with covenant.

I understand, on the contrary, that present political life is not only legitimated from the account of the contract, but also from other forms of bond, that even the contractual side of the political community is recounted in different ways — according to Hobbes, Locke, Kant or Rousseau- and that civil society is not only the kingdom of the covenant, but also that of the interested agreement, that of abuse and injury.

In principle, as far as *politics* is concerned, in this same modern world, in which the idea of the person as a being endowed with the capacity to make agreements has become more compelling and dominant, there are also *other narrations of the contract*, more accurate than that of the Leviathan, for interpreting what the political bonds between citizens *should be like*, if political life wishes to be *legitimate*. Because one thing is to report what is happening, with greater or lesser accuracy, and quite another to state what should happen for a bond — in this case the political one — to be able to claim legitimacy. Political institutions take on legitimacy when they claim to be just, it being precisely the claim to legitimacy which gives them authority to oblige.

With this state of affairs, a notion of the contract such as the Kantian one does not claim to bind together only selfish individuals, led by fear, but persons who are at the same time selfish and morally autonomous, wishing to defend their lives and their property, but in turn concerned with making a community of self-legislating beings possible. The most profound raison d'être of the political community, its goal and meaning, would consist in achieving perpetual peace between peoples and an ethical community, able to gain access to a Kingdom of Ends; a Kingdom in which each human being is treated as an end in him or herself, and not only as a means. The account of the covenant is not very far from this ethical community, and neither is Isaiah's dream — the Prince of Peace — very distant from this political community. The Kingdom of God is not far from either of them. It is indeed at their origin. Today Rawls' political liberalism inherits this idea of the Kantian contract, though slightly weakened, and also sets itself the aim of extending this in some way to all the peoples of the Earth.[13]

What is more, the presence of the Rousseauian *Social Contract*, both in theory and in practice, discredits the idea that there is no contract other than the Hobbesian version. The central importance of the general will, the will expressed by the majority when the whole society seeks common good, exceeds by far the assumptions of an agreement into which the parties only enter through self-interest.

On the other hand, as we pointed out at the beginning of this section, *neither is it acceptable to identify human political capacity with the capacity to contract.* The legitimacy of politics has also been told in other ways, in such a way that its roots sometimes lie in chapters 1 and 2 of Book I of Aristotle's *Politics*, on occasions in the experience of the Roman Republic, and, through different twists and turns (the Italian renaissance cities, Machiavelli, Guicciardini, Rousseau, Paine, the Levellers, Madison, Jefferson), engendering the *republican and communitarian* traditions.

Communitarianism reminds one that the community proves essential for a person's development, including the political community; that ultimately human beings learn to value and decide in communities, as in the political community, communities that cannot be created by means of a contract, but which precede the contract. The Golden Rule as proposed by Amitai Etzioni has its roots in the following principles: "Respect and uphold society's moral order as you would have society respect and uphold your autonomy".[14]

The *republican* traditions on the other hand consider the bonds of civic friendship and cultivation of citizens' virtues to be essential for leading a real political life, these elements already being present in Aristotle's *Politics* and called by Philip Pettit the "intangible hand", through understanding that they

---

[13] J. Rawls, "The Law of Peoples", in *Collected Papers* (ed. by S. Freeman), Cambridge, Harvard University Press, 1999, pp. 529-564). For a more solidarity-based version of Rawls' proposal see E. Martínez, *Solidaridad liberal. La propuesta de John Rawls*, Granada, Comares, 1999.

[14] A. Etzioni, *The New Golden Rule*, New York, Basic Books, XVIII.

coordinate people's action in the political community more appropriately than any liberal "invisible hand".[15] Nevertheless, current republicanism has already drunk from the springs of Modernity, and Modernity consecrates freedom as supreme principle of political life. It is impossible to propose a modern form of politics which turns its back on the idea of freedom. As we have seen in Etzioni's case, the disdain for individual autonomy is unacceptable even for communitarianism.

It nevertheless occurs that freedom, like being, is expressed in many different ways, and it would seem that the development of these forms of freedom has gradually shaped our history: the freedom of the modern, understood as the *"non-arbitrary interference"* of the State or of citizens in people's private life, the freedom of those we could call the "new ancients", understood as participation in the deliberations and decisions about public matters, a specifically republican freedom which, according to Philip Pettit, is expressed as *"non-domination"*, a freedom lastly, to give oneself one's own laws, that is, freedom understood as *autonomy*.

The first of these, freedom as independence, or non-interference, constitutes the most highly-valued asset of liberalism, whilst republican traditions have insisted on participation (Rousseau, Benjamin Barber in *Strong Democracy*), on autonomy (Kant) and on non-domination (Pettit). In any event, to a greater or lesser extent, republicanism understands that the community, the *res publica*, is essential for developing personal freedom, that the social pact of interests is not enough, but that other elements are essential for constructing — as Aristotle would put it — "both house and city". This is so much so that true power in the really political world — Hannah Arendt would say — is communicative power.

Whether these traditions can be considered "republican" or more fittingly be included in the category of "civic humanism" is something that we will comment on further on, but what is true for the time being is that Hobbes' Leviathan is powerless to justify the demands set by societies which, at least verbally, say they wish to be guided by democratic values and boast of having ratified Human Rights' Declarations and Protocols.

Leviathan, as we shall see, cannot govern alone, and needs too much help to be a convincing story as to what human political bonds *should be* like to be legitimate, if we go by the announcements of advanced countries. The figure, as earlier described by Hobbes, is cracked at many points which cry out aloud for other interpretations, other accounts. This is why contemporary moral and political philosophy make every effort to remember other versions of the social

---

[15] Ph. Pettit, R*epublicanism*, Oxford, Oxford University Press, 1997. Pettit does not include Aristotle in the republican category, a point which is quite significant, as will be seen further on.

contract, above all the Kantian version, to update the Aristotelian and Hegelian story of the community and public goods, and to create the intermediate narrations, such as the Habermasian one, of a "deliberative theory" of democracy, which actually have their moral roots in the religious account of the covenant.

3.   Experienced politics, conceived politics

It is nevertheless true that one thing is "conceived politics", and quite a different one is "experienced politics", to take two expressions that José Luis Aranguren very rightly applied to ethics, because if conceived politics is that of the Kantian and Rawlsian contract, that of the community and the res publica, experienced politics, is not even the Hobbesian sort, Leviathan being too large a fit for advanced societies.

Rodrigo Romero, professor of philosophy at the Universidad del Valle, in Cali, said that the great drama of Latin America consists in the fact that the philosophers are Kantian, the constitutions Rawlsian, because they are drawn up by experts sent to Harvard for this purpose, but that the people are Hobbesian, or even less than Hobbesian.

A Hobbesian people, Rodrigo Romero said, would realise that it is in its interests to enter into the political agreement and obey the laws to generate a situation of peace, in which it is possible to live without the fear of death, kidnapping, hold-ups or rape. If they were endowed with intelligence even a people of devils — Kant assured in *Perpetual Peace*, would wish to institute a Constitutional State. And this is the reason why I myself entitled a book *Hasta un pueblo de demonios* ("Even a people of devils"), going by Kant's suggestion, because I understand that even a people of devils would prefer peace to war, cooperation to conflict, mutual help to uncontrolled competitiveness, always on condition that they were intelligent.

But it just so happens that intelligent devils are not easy to find, or rather that the calculation that they make is unlike Hobbes', because Hobbes' proposal had the loose end already mentioned above, that of free ridery. In fact these greedy individuals, craving for all kinds of goods, realise when they get their calculating reason under way that what is really in their interests is not to enter into the agreement and fulfil it, but to enter into it and pretend they are abiding by it, because what is really profitable is that others and not they fulfil the agreement and obey the law. How can one persuade devils to really abide by the contract and not to be satisfied with pretending to comply with it?

There are plenty of theories of rational decision striving precisely to reduce the numbers of free ridery, to design public institutions in such a way that these reinforce virtuous circles in everyone's interest and so that breaking the law is something that proves not to be in individuals' interests.[16] The study of public goods and communal goods, dilemmas such as that of the prisoner, are plentiful in texts on game theories.[17] And nevertheless, it proves difficult for these designs to be successful in practice if this is done without relying on the human capacity to appreciate what is in itself valuable, going beyond the game of self-interest and utility and recognising that there are actions and beings — people — that are worthy in their own right.

This is the approach to a large extent taken by Rawls' and Sen's critiques of utilitarianism, that of raising the theoretical and practical point that there are goods and activities of value for their own sakes, whose value cannot be measured and which are not "useful" for anything. Self-esteem, freedom, the dignity of someone who can come forward in public without being ashamed of him or herself are valuable in themselves.[18] They can clearly be included in the concept of utility, alleging that individuals are interested in these goods, but then we would be extending the concept of utility in such a way that it is no longer good for its intended purpose: providing either cardinal or ordinal measuring units for taking rational decisions on human goods. On the contrary, we human beings often work "for interest", while in other cases we take an "interest in" what is in itself valuable, either an activity, or a being.[19]

Only the experience that there are beings — people — that are in themselves valuable can lead us to understand that it is worthwhile *entering into a covenant with them* and also signing at least a *contract of mutual respect* with them. But one should not forget that the force of the contract, as this is defended in their Constitutions by societies with a liberal democracy, has its roots in the covenant. There is nevertheless, an undeniable schizophrenia between conceived politics and experienced politics. While the first is sustained on the ideas of the Kantian contract, community and deliberation, in "experienced politics" it would instead seem that politics and citizens continue to seek loopholes in Leviathan in their own interests and that only the most powerful and well-informed manage to take real advantage of it. This is why the account of Leviathan continues to be the most fitting one in everyday life for interpreting political and economic ties, and even becomes an almost Utopian account.

---

[16] G. Gutiérrez, *Ética y decisión racional*, Madrid, Síntesis, 2000.

[17] D. Gauthier, *Morals by agreement*, Oxford, Oxford University Press, 1986.

[18] J. Rawls, *A Theory of Justice*, Oxford, Oxford University Press, 1971; A. Sen, *Development as Freedom*, New York, Knopf, 1999.

[19] I. Kant, *Grundlegung zur Metaphysik der Sitten*, IV, chap. 2.

4. Civil society is portrayed in many different ways

As regards the facet of civil society, there can be no doubt that the human being is a social animal "before" being a political animal, in the sense that any human being becomes a person through a process of inter-personal *recognition* and belongs to different associations, one of these being the political community. The person is a member of a family, of a neighbourhood, a group of friends, a professional association, a company, a community of believers, of other civil associations of different kinds and also of a political community, which in the Modern world has customarily taken on the form of national State.

To forget this social nature of the person and reduce all our possible bonds to the political one nevertheless implies a great impoverishment of human associative richness, just as it would also mean an undeniable impoverishment to reduce all possible ties to the economic, family or religious spheres. People have different forms of identity within them, which they share with others until forming that unrepeatable individuality by means of which they are themselves and no-one else.

Nevertheless, identifying the set of ties which are contracted in civil society with the covenant, as told in the book of *Genesis*, is not acceptable, because civil ties are not only ones of the family, friendship, neighbourhood, religion or the ones proper to civic solidarity organisations. Mafias, terrorists and sects also form part of civil society, which is why one should remember from the beginning what can be understood by "civil society", what type of bonds are contracted in this and what their characteristics are, without identifying it immediately with the universe of the covenant (Sacks) or with that of solidarity (Habermas).[20]

In this respect, it is useful to present a double meaning of the term "civil society": a broader sense and a more restricted one. In a *broad sense*, civil society would be characterised as a "mesh of socio-political institutions, which includes a limited government (or State), operating under the dominion of law; a set of social institutions such as markets (or other extensive spontaneous orders) and associations based on voluntary agreements between independent agents, and a public sphere, in which these agents debate in matters of public interest with one another and with the State and commit themselves in public activities".[21]

This would be the type of civil society to which the Scottish philosophers such as Ferguson refer, and the internal meaning of this denomination would

---

[20] I looked into this matter in *Ética aplicada y democracia radical*, Madrid, Tecnos, 1993, chap. 9; "Sociedad civil", in A. Cortina (dir.), *Diez palabras clave en filosofía política*, Estella, Verbo Divino, 1998, pp. 353-388.

[21] V. Pérez Díaz, *La primacía de la sociedad civil*, Madrid, Alianza, 1993, 77; *La esfera pública y la sociedad civil*, Madrid, Taurus, 1997.

consist in this being an already civilised society also made up of citizens (*cives*), not of subjects, which demands that these should be autonomous and for the State to respect their autonomy. A *limited State*, able to respect citizens' independence, is essential to ensure civility, which is why the boundaries between the State and the other social realities which would form civil society understood in the restricted sense are already marked in this concept of civil society.

The *restricted sense* is the customary one today and refers to the social institutions outside the direct control of the State, such as markets, voluntary associations and the world of public opinion. Although not all authors agree to including all these social realities in the notion of civil society, this restricted meaning is now the usual one, and one ought to remember this because, when it is said that any responsible person should assume a social commitment, this is indeed true, but the commitment can be civic or political, depending on the personal vocation.

Nevertheless, recognising that economic concerns, public opinion, civic associations of all kinds and professional activities form part of civil society means in turn admitting that the bonds which tie the members in the different associations in civil society are not always those of the covenant, not even in the majority of cases.

And this is because civil society, like so many other social realities, is portrayed in many different ways. Such authors as Sacks or Habermas exclude the market from civil society and also actually identify this with primary solidarity groups, thus meaning that civil society comes forward as a sort of "remnant of Yahweh", linked by the covenant and reciprocal recognition, the salt of the earth. In my opinion this conception refers more to the "Third Sector" than to civil society.

Indeed, since the nineteen-seventies there has been much talk in industrialised societies of a "Third Sector", in which the population has great hopes. This consists of organisations, civic associations and foundations which are characterised by having solidarity as the supreme reason for their existence. The name is given by the place that this occupies in the institutional structure of industrialised societies with market economy, consisting of at least three sectors: 1) The *Public Sector* ("State"), formed of the Public Authorities. Ultimate control here is in the hands of individuals or groups legitimated by political power and it has public resources. 2) The *Mercantile Private Sector* ("Market"), consisting of the concerns that do business to make a profit and which are controlled by private owners. 3) The *Third Sector or Non-profit-making Private Sector*, also known as "Social Sector", "Independent Sector " and "Third System", whose entities are neither governmental nor have lucrative purposes. Through not coming strictly into the field of Public Law or Private Law these end up being negatively defined, stating that they are neither governmental ("*NGOs*") nor lucrative ("*Non-Profit-Making*"). Nevertheless, it is about time

19

that these were positively characterised for what they are and what they do (*Solidarity Organisations*).

Actually, this scheme would in turn be included in a more simple one, consisting of two sides: State and Civil Society. The *State* has as distinguishing factor the use of coercion, which allows political power, whilst *Civil Society* is the sphere of associations not coerced by the State, some of which have profit-making as a mechanism for offering quality products, while others do so through solidarity.

Identifying civil society with the Third Sector, in which on the other hand it would be necessary to analyse to what point entities such as foundations lie outside the profit area, is as I see it an error, which only creates confusion. This confusion is also found in Benjamin Barber when he proposes his ideal model of civil society as one that allows the person not only to be a voter or consumer, not only to be in the hands of the State or the market. A desirable civil society would be one that deals with public space, and not only that of private life, and constructs this in a participatory way.[22]

As far as I am concerned, I feel that civil society does indeed not have the market as its backbone, as understood by authors such as Black, because this consists also of primary solidarity associations, solidarity organisations and other types of association, both ascriptive and voluntary, as well as public opinion. Nevertheless, markets too are components of civil society, meaning that the Second and Third sectors are combined in this. And what is true is that in a globalised universe it must assume its responsibilities in society as a whole, one of these being the responsibility of exercising the important role which pertains to it; both as far as companies are concerned, as these should assume their corporate responsibility on the international level, and as regards solidarity organisations, above all the ones that already have an international scale.[23]

But — and this should not be forgotten — this is not only the kingdom of the covenant, but also that of the contract and that of group solidarity. One should also remember the account of the covenant and strengthen this, and not only in the spheres in which it proves most difficult to do so (associations of particular interests, markets) but in the spheres which take on all their meaning from this account: family, primary solidarity groups, communities of believers. For in churches too there has also been a prevalence of factions, internal mafias, expulsions, rights, promotions, career-seeking, and everything proper to an institution reflecting its origins very dimly. In the beginning there was the

---

[22] B. Barber, *A Place for Us*, New York, Farrar, Straus and Giroux, 1998.

[23] G. Enderle, "Business and Corporate Ethics in the USA: Philosophy and Practice", in B.N. Kumar/H. Steinmann (eds.), *Ethics in International Management*, Walter de Gruyter, Berlin-New York, 1998, pp. 367-400; G. Enderle (ed.), International Business Ethics, Notre Dame, University of Notre Dame Press, 1999.

covenant, with God and with others, In the beginning there was mercy and compassion.

5.   Politics, ethics and religion

From what has been said so far it follows that the two types of bond which unite human beings and which enable them to overcome structural violence or particular outbreaks of this are not split between the two parts of society, State and civil society, but are instead mixed up in both of them, in such a way, as we shall see further on, that ultimately the political pact takes on its meaning from reciprocal recognition and civil society also requires contracts.

But it is also true that our two parables give rise to three, similarly entwined, dimensions of the person: the political, ethical and religious facets. Curiously, the ethical dimension too, and not only the political one, has been understood in the past and is still understood as being the product of a contract from the standpoint of all the theories that believe, with Hobbes and Gauthier, that moral standards are reached by agreement. "Before" the agreement there are no political norms, but neither are there moral ones, and just as juridical laws are the result of a treaty of self-interest, so are moral standards.

Other traditions, to which I myself would subscribe, maintain on the contrary that moral norms are born from recognition between subjects, that the basic core of social life is the *inter-subjective* relationship, which extends, we would say today, to all those who are endowed with communicative competence. This would be the basis for a civic ethics, the core of a global ethics, through whose veins flows the secularised blood of the covenant.[24] This is the *proper foundation for civic ethics*, which imbues liberal societies, and that of a global ethics, while the "morality by agreement", in any of its versions, is not worthy of the name of "ethics". What actually occurs is that particular norms, the ethical codes from the different social spheres (bioethics, GenEthics, ecoethics, "infoethics", companies, solidarity organisations, etc.), have to be established by agreement after a process of deliberation, but the principles and values which give them a meaning and legitimacy are not the object of an agreement. This is why civic ethics lies "between the covenant and the contract".

And as regards religion, if we refer to the Jewish and Christian faiths, what doubt can there be that the covenant is the ground that nurtures them and their vital project? What doubt can there be that these are being ill-used and perverted

---

[24] J. Conill, "Teoría de la acción comunicativa como filosofía de la religión", in *Estudios filosóficos*, n° 128 (1996), pp. 55-73; J. Habermas, *Vom sinnlichen Eindruck zum symbolischen Ausdruck*, Frankfurt, Suhrkamp, 1997.

when they are used as a platform for power or a weapon? What doubt is there that the triumph of Canon Law in the religious sphere is a genuine failure,[25] because its voice is that of justice, born from compassion.

6. The voice of justice and the voice of compassion

In this respect, it is important to remember that in the end, psychologist Carol Gilligan altered the approach of her master Lawrence Kohlberg, showing him that in the moral sphere it is not a single voice, that of justice, that is heard, but also a quieter voice, that of compassion. The story goes more or less like this.

Kohlberg conceived a doctrine of moral development according to which people's moral conscience gradually evolves through stages of maturity, which are the same in all human beings.[26] Using the technique of giving subjects moral dilemmas with very precise questionnaires, designed to appraise the subjects' argumentation level, Kohlberg analysed the structure of the person's moral growth taking into account how they came to judgements on the justice of acts. The conclusion was as follows: the formation of moral judgements is developed through certain stages, in which it is possible to establish a sequence of 3 levels and 6 stages (2 for each level) from infancy to the adult age.

On the first of the three levels, on the pre-conventional level, the individual takes egoism as the principle of justice: understanding that what is just is what suits him. On the conventional level, obviously the second one, the person approaches moral questions in accordance with the standards, expectations and interests suiting the "established social order" because it is above all of interest to him to be accepted by the group, and to this end he is willing to obey its customs; taking what conforms to the standards and customs of his society as being just. On the third level, the post-conventional one, the person distinguishes between the standards of his society and universal moral principles, approaching moral problems from the latter standpoint.

On this level there are two stages which should be borne in mind for the purposes of the present discussion. In theory, what is just is defined according to the rights, values and legal contracts constitutionally and democratically recognised by society as a whole. Legality also rests on rational calculations of social

---

[25] On the situation of religion in the "secular city" see, amongst others, the works of H. Cox, *Religion in the Secular City*, New York, Simon & Schuster, 1984; G. Amengual, *Presencia elusiva*, Madrid, PPC, 1996; Ll. Duch, *Religión y mundo moderno*, Madrid, PPC, 1995; J. Martín Velasco, *Ser cristiano en una cultura posmoderna*, Madrid, PPC, 1996; J.L. Ruiz de la Peña, *Una fe que crea cultura*, Madrid, Caparrós, 1997.

[26] L. Kohlberg, Ch. Levine, A. Hewer, Moral Stages: A Current Formulation and a Response to Critics, New York, S. Karger, 1983; V. Gozálvez, *Inteligencia moral*, Bilbao, Desclée de Brouwer, 2000.

utility ("the greatest good for the largest number possible"). Later on, the person may go beyond the contractual and utilitarian viewpoint to think from the standpoint of ethical principles of justice valid for the whole of humanity. The question is one of recognising human rights in equality and respect for the personal dignity of all human beings. What is just is defined now by the decision of the conscience in accordance with such principles. The conquest of autonomy is thus considered as being the target of the person's moral development. According to Kohlberg, this level is the less frequently found one, arising during adolescence or in the early adult age and characterises the reasoning of only a minority of adults.

As we shall see, from an ethical standpoint contractualism still has its shortcomings. What is morally just is not only what we agree to in particular communities, but what we would extend to all human beings according to universalist principles.

Nevertheless, as Gilligan would say, this is one form of understanding ethics, but there are others. The ethics of justice must be complemented by the ethics of care.

Indeed, in their research work both Kohlberg and other relevant psychologists (Freud and Piaget) use only males and not females, and furthermore western males, born in liberal democracies. As a large number of women do not respond to their research as they would wish to back up their hypotheses, they conclude that women display a "deviant" conduct instead of recognising that this behaviour is simply different.[27]

This is why Gilligan endeavoured to make some tests with women, presenting them moral dilemmas to which they had to give reasoned solutions, and reached the conclusion that there are two different languages for codifying the moral world. Two languages that are not subordinated, but that one of these has made itself heard more than the other: the language of the logic of the impartiality of justice, which consists in making decisions by putting oneself in the place of any other, and the language of the psychological logic of relations, which assumes the perspective of the concrete situation, and attempts to preserve the relations already created.

A comparison can be established between both languages allowing an analysis of which values are given greater weight by each of these.

---

[27] C. Gilligan, *In a Different Voice*, Cambridge Mass, Harvard University Press, 1982.

Logic of justice (Separation)	Logic of care (Union)
Individualisation	Meshing relations which could be damaged
Autonomy	Protecting what is vulnerable (relations, the weak)
Law/Rights/Justice	Responsibility/Care
Contract	Protection/Self-sacrifice
Abstraction	Narration/Context
Universality	Particularity
Impartiality	Partiality

From this standpoint, the values appreciated in the "masculine language" would be the ones which gradually form independent individuals, able to make decisions about what is just and what is unjust from impartial conditions. On the other hand, the values preferred by "feminine language" will be the ones which protect human relations, take care of the weak, and care for particular persons in specific contexts of action.

Nevertheless, this does not mean that males have to opt for autonomy and justice, and women for care and compassion. Such a distribution of roles and values always acts to the detriment of both sexes, because the four ingredients mentioned (justice, autonomy, compassion and responsibility) are essential for reaching moral maturity. For one or another to predominate in a person is thus an individual question, rather than a characteristic of the sex as a whole.

What happens instead is that there are at least *two moral voices*, in which both women and men have to express themselves: 1) The voice of justice, which consists in judging about good and bad from a universal standpoint, beyond social conventions and group gregariousness. This perspective is given the name of "impartiality". 2) The voice of compassion for those who need help, who are our own responsibility, starting with the closest ones.

The voice of compassion has been heard little, according to Gilligan. The parable of the covenant, Sacks complained, has been pushed to one side by that of the contract, and furthermore — we ourselves should add — by that of the Leviathan contract, signed by selfish individuals, who cannot dream of any justice beyond that of Kohlberg's stage five in the best of cases. Because the voice of justice, based on really universal principles, is more widely heard in announcements ("conceived politics") than it is put into practice in everyday life ("experienced politics").

It is thus vital to go on telling those accounts of the person's holiness, of their dignity, which is the basis of demandable justice. It is essential to go on recounting the stories of the covenant, of mutual recognition, which are the basis from which each person is given what they need to have life, and to have plentiful life.

II. Leviathan's inability to govern alone

3. FISSURES IN THE POLITICAL CONTRACT

1. The original freedoms

As has already been mentioned, when the legitimacy of the State, the emerging political configuration is being considered, not only Hobbes, but also a good deal of modern moral and political philosophy has this rest on the idea of social agreement between individuals, endowed with rational rights and with the capacity to contract. It is thus understood in theory that the contract is sealed by independent beings, empowered to establish agreements and with the ability to exchange something; loyalty to the State in exchange for protection of rights. This demonstrates that the modern world has its roots in the idea of *exchange*, whether this be economic or political, and that whoever has nothing to offer in exchange is indeed in a poor way in this world.[1]

The Constitutional State, characterised by being governed by rule of law, thus grows from the idea of the agreement. Nevertheless, the fact that the law should hold sway is justified because it is intended to defend a set of rights which will in time be extended. Satisfying these rights will be a *requirement of justice*, which will gradually be implemented in more and more spheres of social life and of human necessities.

In theory, these are the *rights* or *"basic liberties"* that a liberal such as Benjamin Constant characterises as follows: "For each of them it is the right to be subjected only to the laws, and to be neither arrested, detained, put to death or maltreated in any way by the arbitrary will of one or more individuals. It is the right of everyone to express their opinion, choose a profession and practice it, to dispose of property, and even to abuse it; to come and go without permission, and without having to account for their motives or undertakings. It is everyone's right to associate with other individuals, either to discuss their interests, or to profess the religion which they and their associates prefer, or even simply to occupy their days or hours in a way which is most compatible with their inclinations or whims. Finally it is everyone's right to exercise some influence on the administration of the government, either by electing all or particular officials, or through representations, petitions, demands to which the authorities are more or less compelled to pay heed ".[2]

---

[1] A. Cortina, *Hasta un pueblo de demonios*, Introduction.
[2] B. Constant, "De la liberté des Anciens comparées à celle des Modernes", 1815.

These rights are intended to express an idea of liberty which Constant himself called the "liberty of the modern" and also *"liberty understood as independence"*, because exercising these rights allows each citizen to be independent of the others and to be free of State interference. This is the freedom which individuals have defended with greatest zeal from the beginnings of Modernity to our own times, as opposed to other forms of understanding freedom, as participation ("liberty of the ancients"), as non-domination, or as autonomy. Setting oneself laws, being governed by one's own criteria, is a genuinely arduous business.[3]

Obviously, the State which assumes this task is gradually configured as a liberal Constitutional State, created precisely to defend above all basic liberties, as befits the liberal world. It does not therefore matter what the *historical origin* of the social agreement is, what matters is that its *rational justification*, its *sufficient reason,* should lie in defending the human rights or basic liberties which we have mentioned in Constant's words.

And precisely because the political community is born with the mission of protecting these rights for its citizens, the idea of "citizenship" gradually takes on the sense of *"civil and political citizenship"*: one is a citizen in a political community if one finds in this protection for one's civil rights and political participation, which will later be considered as being "first generation rights".

2. Fissures in the social contract

In spite of the protection of these rights being the legitimising principle of the political community, one should nevertheless reflect on the fact with which we are concerned in this book, that *it is not the contract itself which founds the rights*, but that, for the agreement to have a meaning, a large number of suppositions "prior" to the agreement have to be accepted. These premises act as cracks through which the conviction that *the contract is not self-sufficient, but needs to rest on the mutual recognition founded by the covenant,* gradually but inevitably slips.

For the political agreement to have a meaning, at least *six assumptions*, six fissures have to be admitted at this level of first generation rights:

1) The *first* of the suppositions for an agreement to have a meaning is that of recognising *"agreements must be observed"* as being a moral duty and that this duty is not proper to positive law, but a moral or religious premise of positive law.

---

[3] A. Cortina, *Ciudadanos del mundo*, chap. VII.

Indeed, Hobbes himself classifies the law that men should comply with agreements that they have sealed as being one of the "laws of nature",[4] and this is one of the weakest points of his proposal, because apart from the concept of the "law of nature" being extremely ambiguous, it proves obvious that someone who enters into an agreement solely through self-interest will drop this as soon as it is of interest to him, and that the idea that "agreements are to be observed" is either a moral supposition of the agreements themselves, or there is no meaning whatsoever in obeying this when the agreement fails to be in one's interests. Centuries later Karl-Otto Apel would remind those upholding the self-sufficiency of positive law that without the moral supposition *"pacta sunt servanda"*, positive law has no base.[5]

2) *Secondly*, for agreements to have a meaning it is necessary for relations of *trust* to exist between those who sign them. They not only have to *know* that they are under the law that agreements are to be complied with, but have to be able to *trust* in their being complied with. Without trust in the compliance of mercantile, matrimonial, political or any other sort of contracts, the whole universe of agreements is deprived of its foundations.

The warning made by Francis Fukuyama that it is necessary to generate and strengthen trust between people, if we want human exchanges, including economic ones, to survive and work properly, becomes really lucid in this respect, stating that "if the institutions of democracy and capitalism are to work properly, they must coexist with certain pre-modern cultural habits,[6] which ensure their proper operation. Laws, contracts and economic rationality provide foundations that are necessary but not sufficient to maintain the stability and prosperity of post-industrial societies; it is also necessary for them to count on reciprocity, moral obligations, responsibility for the community and trust, which is based more on a habit than on a rational calculation. This trust does not constitute an anachronism for modern society, but instead the *sine qua non* for its success".[7]

Trust thus forms part of that "social capital" of values which members of a society have to rely on in order to build their lives together and which cannot be agreed on, but which have to be presupposed in social relations.[8]

---

[4] Th. Hobbes, *Leviathan*, chap. 15.

[5] K.-O. Apel, "¿Lässt sich ethische Vernunft von strategischer Zweckrationalität unterscheiden? Zum Problem der Rationalität sozialer Kommunikation und Interaktion", Archivio di Filosofia, LI (1983), 375-434 A. Cortina, *Ética mínima*, Madrid, Tecnos, 1986, chap. 4.

[6] Considering such habits as being "pre-modern" is unwise, as J. Conill shows in "Reconfiguración ética del mundo laboral", in A. Cortina (dir.), *Rentabilidad de la ética para la empresa*, Madrid, Fundación Argentaria/Editorial Visor, 1997, pp. 187-228.

[7] F. Fukuyama, *Trust*, New York, The Free Press, 1995, p. 11.

[8] R. Putnam, *Making Democracy Work*, Princeton University Press,1993; F. Fukuyama, *The Great Disruption*, New York, The Free Press, 1999. See chap. 6 of this same book.

3) Thirdly, the apparent self-sufficiency of the contract for legitimating the validity of legal-political standards rests on the effectiveness of atomism in the political sphere. But —Taylor will say — rights never have priority over the society to which an individual belongs, not even human rights, because rights are the result of *evaluations*. The western world values the practice of certain capacities, through considering these to be essential to live a really human life, in such a way that it protects their practice, assuring that this constitutes an inviolable "human right", a "moral right", prior to any agreement. Nevertheless, other societies which give a higher priority to other capacities will not rate these so highly. This is why society and its valuations can be said to be "prior" to the individual and his or her rights. Defending rights requires making society itself responsible for the tradition of rights not to be extinguished.

From this the "New Golden Rule" that Etzioni proposes would follow, no longer interpersonal like the traditional Golden Rule ("Do not do to others what you do not want them to do to you", or, "Do as you would be done by"), but instead tying the individual to the community.

4) Nevertheless, it is true that the tradition of human rights was born in the western world, from the valuation of certain capacities for leading a fully human life, but it is also true that this tradition formally claims universality, through considering that questions of good life are extremely personal, but questions of justice are not. The expression "this is fair" formally claims universality, which is why any argumentation on questions of justice requires the dialogue of all those affected by this. And dialogue, to have a meaning, demands the premise of pragmatic and moral rights. These rights are not the object of the agreement, but are recognised as what gives meaning to the act of entering into the agreement.

5) Indeed, human rights *are not the object of the agreement*, not the object of the contract, not agreed on, but recognised as what gives meaning to the act of entering into the agreement. Obviously what gives meaning to the contract cannot be the object of a contract. This is the reason why in certain traditions human rights are expressly called "*moral rights*", to distinguish them clearly from what we could call "legal rights".

6) Lastly, the obligation to protect these rights takes on its binding force from the mutual recognition, as valid interlocutors, of all beings able to establish contracts. This is why political communities, though they are in theory obliged to protect their citizens, are also necessarily open to all human beings. That is, these necessarily have a cosmopolitan vocation.

3. Human rights are not the object of the agreement

The term *"human rights"* is closely linked with other well-known expressions, such as "natural rights", "moral rights", "fundamental rights", or some not so well-known terms, such as "subjective public rights" or "public freedoms".[9] It has the advantage of being the most popular of all of these, through having been used by the United Nations as a label in the Universal Declaration of 1948, as well as immediately showing that these rights can only be claimed by human beings, but indeed, by each and every one of us.

As regards their *historical origin*, human rights are born from natural rights, with their roots in the Natural Law of stoic and Christian traditions, which are undoubtedly universalist traditions. While in classical Athens the statement that the citizen is a free being does not go beyond the sphere of the *polis* — and even there, women, children, slaves and *metekos*, "through their own nature" have no freedom — stoic and above all Christian universalism gradually extend an asset to each human being: that of being endowed with rights which pertain to them through being a person. This *"holiness"* of the person, which was spoken about in the book of *Genesis* and which later on would be translated in a secular version as *dignity*, lies at the roots of those rights which are in theory known as natural.

This is the universalism which takes hold in modern reason, the ground in which Modernity's rational iusnaturalism takes root. Precisely, when reflecting on the legitimacy of political power, Hobbes and Locke, Pufendorf, Kant and the other contractualists understand that its legitimacy proceeds from the pact sealed to protect these rational natural rights, which later on will be given the name of "human rights" to avoid the problems which may arise if the adjective "natural" is kept.

Indeed, committing oneself to the expression "natural rights" may lead to a number of ambiguities. The first of these would consist in believing that nature sets some species over others and for this reason gives some species rights and not others. Humanity's task would consist in discovering these rights given by nature, and it would thus ensue that human beings have not until now been able to discover any rights other than the ones granted by nature to human beings themselves, whilst in recent times the discovery has been made that animals too have been privileged by nature with rights, which their greatest enthusiasts are bold enough to describe as "human" rights, incurring at the very least in a semantic contradiction.

---

[9] I dealt with this matter in other works such as "Derechos humanos y discurso político", in G. González (coord.), *Derechos humanos. La condición humana en la sociedad tecnológica*, Madrid, Tecnos, 1999, pp. 36-55.

Nevertheless, as Kant so rightly said at least two centuries ago, nature does not display any greater delicacy with some beings than with others, because natural phenomena affect men in the same way as other beings.[10] In spite of ecologists' enthusiasm for proclaiming that it is human intervention in nature which has distorted this to such an extent that it often acts destructively for men, it is nonetheless true that from the very beginning volcanoes, landslides, earthquakes or cyclones have harmed the different species with no exceptions. Nature does not distinguish some beings from others, and does not give some rights and deny these to others.

Clearly, we are not using the expression "natural rights" to refer to rights given by physical nature, but by a Nature which acts intelligently and expresses its will in Natural Law. The difficulty then lies, first of all, in elucidating if what we mean with this Nature that works to ends is in fact a Creative God, who directs all beings towards their own good, in which case non-believers would have no reason to recognise natural rights, and believers would have to wonder who the authorised interpreters of Natural Law might be. However, if the medieval world and the Scholastic tradition understood that the faithful interpreters of Natural Law were the natural reason of all men and also the Magisterium of the Church, the iusnaturalista philosophers of the Modern age placed the task of interpreting the Natural Law from which natural rights are recognized in the domain of natural reason. This transfer nevertheless also failed to clear up the many problems posed by Natural Law.

For iusnaturalism, even the philosophical sort, was not free of problems[11] either, amongst other reasons, because its basic assumption involved considering that there are two legal orders, the natural and the positive forms, and that positive law norms are only "valid rights" when they conform to Natural Law, and are not "by right" if they do not conform to this. As has so rightly been shown, amongst others, by Carlos Nino, for a norm to be legally valid, that is, for it to be "by right", it is enough for it to have been promulgated by the procedures required for this purpose.[12] It is quite another matter that the norm may be unjust: the *legal validity* of a positive law norm does not imply that this is *just*.[13] It would thus be preferable to talk of "human rights" rather than "natural rights", to avoid this type of ambiguities and properly establish that these rights refer only to people, and not to other types of beings.

However, it is indeed true that human rights are extremely peculiar, because they do not belong to the category of "legal rights", covered in positive codes,

---

[10] I. Kant, *Kritik der Urteilskraft*, V, paragraph 82.

[11] For the different versions of iusnaturalism see, amongst others, A.E. Pérez Luño, *Derechos humanos, Estado de Derecho y Constitución*, Madrid, Tecnos, 1984, chap. 1; J. Ballesteros, *Sobre el sentido del derecho*, Madrid, Tecnos, 1994.

[12] C.S. Nino, *Ética y derechos humanos*, Buenos Aires, Barcelona, Mexico, Paidós, 1984.

[13] E. Díaz, *Ética contra política*, Madrid, Centro de Estudios Constitucionales, 1990, 17-64.

but to a type of rights somehow "prior" to this type of codes. "Prior" means that these are not rights that political communities graciously grant, but that the communities which assume them *recognise* that human beings have such rights. This is the reason why a thriving Anglo-Saxon tradition calls them *"moral rights"*, ones which should inspire the preparation of constitutional texts and concrete legislations, meaning that these are not rights which "are granted", but which *"are recognised"* for those who have them, through being persons.

The existence of this type of rights has been denied by some western moral and political philosophical traditions.

Jeremy Bentham, one of the founders of Utilitarianism, considered these to be "nonsense on stilts" because, in his eyes "there is no right which, when the abolition of it is advantageous to society, should not be abolished".[14] Nietzsche and his followers understand that human rights constitute one of the ramifications of the "shadow of God" and thus constitute an obstacle for the "Great Politics" which would prepare the advent of Superman,[15] and they are not so far wrong, to the extent that the idea of man being made in God's image and likeness continues to pervade the human holiness and dignity which gives the recognition of human rights its foundation. Authors of our own times, such as Alasdair MacIntyre, explicitly affirm that the aforementioned rights are useful fiction or fables, as devoid of existence as witches or unicorns.[16]

These categorical denials in my view originate in the ambiguous nature of human rights, but this ambiguity may vanish if we realize that they are actually primarily *moral demands* to lead a human life, to which we give the name of "rights" to stress that there is a duty to comply with these. The *radical nature of human rights is thus that of moral exigencies which any human being possesses and which must be satisfied by human beings, if they wish to measure up to their humanity.*

Nevertheless, this statement does not answer all the questions posed about with human rights either, but leaves at least four open:
1) Why are certain needs of human beings interpreted as moral exigencies which, in the form of rights, must be complied with by other human beings? This is evidently the question about the foundations of human rights.
2) Which of these needs must be "converted" into rights that have to be protected and which do not?
3) Why should anyone feel obliged to fulfil these demands even without any agreement whatsoever having been sealed?

---

[14] "Anarchical Fallacies", in J. Waldron (ed.), *Nonsense on Stilts: Bentham, Burke and Marx on the Rights of Man*, London, New York, Methuen, 1987, 53.

[15] J. Conill, *El poder de la mentira. Nietzsche y la política de la transvaloración*, Madrid, Tecnos, 1997.

[16] A. MacIntyre, *After Virtue*, chap. 6.

4) Who should protect people's rights, bearing in mind that each and every person has these?

This last question forces us today to look beyond the frontiers of the national state and involve a Cosmopolitan Republic in this task, a republic not only made up of national States (in that case it would be "International"), but also, and very particularly, of these Solidarity Organisations which have for a long time been working with cosmopolitan intentions and reality.[17] I prefer to call them "Solidarity Civic Organisations", rather than use the negative term "Non-Governmental Organisations", because it does not seem to me that designating social realities by what they are not (non-governmental) leads one very close to their meaning.

And to get back to human rights, it is thus not surprising with this state of affairs that the Universal Declaration of Human Rights of 1948 should on occasions have been considered as being a *"moral code"*, and that the problem of its legal validity has been widely debated. The most widespread conviction in this respect is that the rights recognized half a century ago by the United Nations are the moral exigencies that become principles of law for civilized nations.

It therefore seems to be openly admitted that human rights are premises for social agreements, which means that they are not the object of the contract, and so the question "why should anyone have to feel themselves obliged to satisfy these demands if no agreement whatsoever has been signed?" could be answered with another question: *"might it not be that we are in fact assuming the existence of a human bond prior to the agreement, also for recognizing what we call "human rights" in other beings?*

Before attempting to reply to this question, and to the others that have been left open, we will go on to consider how in the case of the so-called "second-generation", or "economic, social and cultural" rights, the contract by which Leviathan is fashioned also proves to be insufficient and needs to involve assumptions involving a non-contractual form of bond.

4. THE HISTORY OF JUSTICE

1. Narrations of human history

The range of human rights has gradually grown over time, and articles 22 to 26 of the United Nations' 1948 Universal Declaration of Human Rights thus

---

[17] D. Held, *Democracy and the global order*, London, Polity Press, 1995.

also mention a "second generation of rights", the so-called "social rights", characterising these as being "economic, social and cultural rights". These are essentially the right to social security, to work and all that this involves, rest, food, clothing, housing, medical care and social services, to insurance at vulnerable times of life (unemployment, illness, disability, widowhood, old age, etc.) and to education.

Claiming the status of rights for these needs was not an exigency of philosophers, economists and liberal politicians, who were above all concerned with defending civil liberties and the possibility of taking part in the government of the political community. Liberalism, in its different varieties, has displayed greater interest in defending legal and political citizenship than defending "social citizenship". It was above all the socialist movements which fought for recognition of social citizenship, but what is definitely true is that the idea of citizenship seen in the Constitutions of most European and Latin American states is that of social citizenship, proposed in the mid-nineteenth century by Thomas S. Marshall.

From this standpoint, a *citizen* is a person whose rights are *recognised and protected* in their political community, not only their *civil and political rights, but also "economic, social and cultural ones"*.[18]

Nevertheless, social rights suffer from at least a double weakness. In theory, respect and protection of these seem less demandable than those of first generation rights through corresponding to the type of duties which have been given the name of "imperfect duties" and secondly, through seeming the most difficult to realise, given the critical situation in which the Welfare State that sheltered these finds itself. In my opinion, however, social rights are at least *as demandable* as civil and political rights and are furthermore *realisable*, on condition that the Welfare State becomes a *State of Justice*, willing to protect *active social citizenship*.[19]

Still, to be able to make such a statement, humanity has had to wend its way through a long history which can be construed in many different ways and can also be recounted in different ways. One of these ways, the approach I am putting forward in this book, would consist in interpreting the history of the West as the progressive realisation of the idea of Justice, with rights which were once understood as being needs that had to be satisfied by *charity*, not by justice, having gradually been recognised as rights which have to be dealt with *in justice*, meaning that those who do not fulfil them consequently drop under minima of justice.

This is a rather different form of "telling" human history to Hegel's. But before going on to tell the story, I should like to add that *there is a type of*

---

[18] T.H. Marshall, *Citizenship and Social Class*, London, Pluto Press 1992.
[19] Adela Cortina, *Ciudadanos del mundo*, chap. 3.

human needs which can never demand to be satisfied in justice, because nobody will ever be able to have the *duty* of meeting these. And these are not "obligations of beneficence": they are the type of needs that only someone who feels essentially bonded to the needy feels obliged to fulfil *gratuitously*. *Gratuity is not the same as beneficence.*

This story is thus, amongst others, the history of Justice and Gratuity, but this will be dealt with in the last part of this book.

2.   From Beneficence to Justice

In his *Principles of the Philosophy of Law*, Hegel attempted to reconstruct the history of humanity as the gradual realisation of liberty. At the beginning of this history there was the *Lógos*, which is reason and word, there was the relationship between human subjects who, through recognising each other as such, set out together on the common road of freedom. As opposed to the liberal contractualism which we spoke about at the start of this book, which insists on the root having been the individual with his natural rights at the beginning, with the desire to seal an agreement to submit to joint law coming later on, Hegel,[20] incorporating the tradition of the covenant, understands that the basic category from which the human world is fashioned is not that of the "*individual with his rights*", but that of "*reciprocal recognition between subjects*". Later on, social psychologist G.H. Mead would also approach this key of reciprocal recognition and end up by affirming that "we are what we are thanks to our relations with others".[21] Interpersonal relationships, in the context of a political community, of whatever sort this may be, lie at the beginning and end of history, at the alpha and omega.

Turning to the matter of human rights from this standpoint, could we not say instead that man's history is that of the realisation of the idea of *Justice*, and that we are gradually recognising certain demands seeming originally to have been *invitations to beneficence* as *demands of justice*?

It does tend to be said that civil and political rights are guided by the desire to realise personal liberty, which is the dream of liberalism, while social rights would tend to achieve a greater equality, or to reduce inequalities, which is the aim of socialism. In any event, what is certainly true is that it proves impossible to take a society as being just if in such society all do not enjoy freedom or if all cannot make similar use of having this, both of these being impossible without a determined protection of social rights.

---

[20] G.W.F. Hegel, *Grundlinien der Philosophie des Rechts*, Par. 75, Added.
[21] G.H. Mead, *Mind, Self and Society*, Chicago, University of Chicago Press.

But the fact is nevertheless the case that social rights were born handicapped with the difficulty of corresponding to "imperfect obligation" duties, while the ones corresponding to civil and political rights were "perfect obligation" duties.[22]

In the tradition of rational iusnaturalism *perfect duties* are the ones that have to be obeyed without leaving any room for exceptions, because they are seen as *demands of justice* which have to be satisfied without exception. These are duties which are normally formulated negatively and which are intended to ensure respect for people's independence. If we go by Constant's view, according to which the modern world appreciates freedom understood as independence above all else, it is not surprising that the duties of non-interference in others' lives and anything protecting the independence of those lives should be considered as being perfect.

Imperfect or wide obligation duties are on the other hand ones that oblige, whilst leaving room for exceptions, because these are in theory positive duties, "*duties of beneficence*", which would seem to have two characteristic traits: they may come into collision with others, and no-one can point out to what extent these are universally demandable. To what extent should a person help their neighbour? To what extent should the State seek the welfare of its citizens? To what extent should international organisations strive for each and every person's "wellbeing"? Indeed, nobody can point out *a priori* any universally demandable yardstick for these, which makes imperfect obligations discretionary. Ultimately, it can always be said that these duties oblige to the extent to which complying with them does not start to cause detriment to the person obliged by them, though this point is understandably open to interpretation.

As regards social rights, these seem to underlie imperfect duties, whose degree of compliance is discretional, because performance of these duties requires positive action; secondly, because such positive action may lead the state to interfering in people's private lives; and thirdly, because complying with these duties also requires investing resources, which are always scarce, and they thus entail the implementation of an order of priorities.

The first and third aspect of the three mentioned above is dealt with in article 22 of the 1948 Universal Declaration of Human Rights, which is formulated as follows: "Everyone, as a member of society, has the right to social security and is entitled to realization, through national effort and international co-operation *and in accordance with the organization and resources of each State*, of the economic, social and cultural rights indispensable for his dignity and the free development of his personality".[23]

---

[22] I. Kant, *Grundlegung zur Metaphysik der Sitten*, IV. chap. 2; *Metaphysik der Sitten, VI* pp. 390 ff.
[23] My underlining.

The expression "in accordance with the organisation and resources of each State" makes the degree of realisation of these rights depend on the resources available in each State and on the order of priorities introduced by the corresponding authority. This seems reasonable in theory, but involves the disadvantage of leaving the decision about the degree to which these rights can be covered in the hands of this authority, which does not always coincide with what is really possible.

To make the matter more complicated, decisions in these cases cannot be made by each national State independently of other States and peoples today because, in the same way as the first principle of ecology reminds us of the interdependence of all parts of the planet, the first principle of a globalised universe also points out the interdependence of States and peoples. Each of these increasingly depends on decisions of this type of transnational units and as a background framework, on the world horizon. Computerised and financial globalisation unquestionably demand a review of international economic relations.[24]

3. A cosmopolitan community

Indeed, one of the great questions posed about the first two generation human rights is that of who is obliged to satisfy them. As regards first and second generation rights, we said that the national State is the party having this obligation, but such an affirmation means leaving at least two loose ends.

National States can appeal to article 22 of the 1948 Universal Declaration and allege that they cannot satisfy all citizens' social rights because they lack the resources required for this, that the protection of such rights is an ideal towards which one has to head, but not an exigency which can be accomplished.

And as regards basic freedoms, National States can shelter behind law in force to leave even crimes against humanity unpunished, on the grounds that certain political posts are immune from judicial procedures and corresponding punishments. The case of Augusto Pinochet has been a sufficiently eloquent example of the difference existing, as I stated elsewhere, between "conducting Law" and "doing justice".[25]

---

[24] U. Beck, *Was ist Globalisierung? Frankfurt, Suhrkamp, 1997*; H.P. Martin/H. Schumann, *Die Globalisierungsfalle*, Reinbek bei Hamburg, Rowohlt, 1996; J. García Roca, "Globalización. Un mundo único, desigual y antagónico", in A. Cortina (dir.), *Diez palabras clave en filosofía política*, Estella, VD, 1998, pp. 163-212; S. Amin, *El capitalismo en la Era de la Globalización*, Barcelona, Paidós, 1999; G. De la Dehesa, *Para comprender la globalización*, Madrid, Alianza, 2000.

[25] A. Cortina, "Justicia global y local", in *El País*, 17-XI-98.

The attempt to try General Pinochet and the trial of Milosevic have indeed brought up for discussion the urgency of seriously tackling the institutionalisation of a global justice, which has clear antecedents in the Nürenberg trials after the Second World War. In that particular case the debt owed to the concentration camp martyrs was doubtlessly not settled, but human beings can only condemn past, avoid present and foresee future injustice, one reason why it is necessary to develop the International Penal Court which has already been founded and increase its competences so that any who require this can resort to it with all due confidence in being properly treated. But even so, though it is necessary, it is not enough. The courts and the laws are clearly insufficient when not *conducting Law*, but *doing Justice* is involved.

Citizens have to become accustomed to doing justice in everyday life, but the foundations for a cosmopolitan citizenship must also be laid, with the aid of such international courts, with agreements between States and the work of these Civic Organisations which have for a long time been forging global solidarity networks, converting the universal *res publica* little by little into something involving all human beings. Achieving global justice demands a long apprenticeship in the school of *cosmopolitan citizenship* which should in questions of justice have priority over national citizenship.

But what is more, the number of "generations of rights" has, as we already know, been extended over time to a *third* and occasionally a fourth generation. The *third generation* package includes the right to peace,[26] to a healthy environment, both as regards pollution and noise, and the right to peoples' development.[27]

The *fourth generation* would involve rights made pressing through technical progress (intimacy of genetic heritage, freedom in computer technology etc.)[28] or for the "struggles for recognition" carried out by certain groups (feminists, homosexuals, etc.). Since this fourth generation is not well-defined, it is advisable to refer above all to the first three and observe how their satisfaction demands transcending the frontiers of national States.

The third generation is indeed said to be guided by the value of solidarity, while the two previous ones stood under the flag of freedom and equality, respectively, but the most important point to stress on the matter now concerning us involves three characteristics of the rights of which this consists:

---

[26] V. Martínez, "Paz", in A. Cortina (dir.), *Diez palabras clave en filosofía política*, pp. 309-352; *Hacer las Paces*, Barcelona, Icaria, 2001.

[27] D. Goulet, *Ética del Desarrollo*, Barcelona, IEPAL-Estela, 1965; *The Cruel Choice: A New Concept in the Theory of Development*, New York, Atheneum, 1971; *Ética del Desarrollo*, IEPALA, 1999; D. Crocker, "Toward Development Ethics", in *World Development*, n. 19 (1991), pp. 457-483; E. Martínez, *Ética para el desarrollo de los pueblos*, Madrid, Trotta, 2000; A. Sen, *Development as Freedom*.

[28] G. González (coord.), *Derechos humanos. La condición humana en la sociedad tecnológica*, Parte II: "Sociedad Tecnológica y Derechos humanos".

1) These are rights whose realisation is *conditio sine qua non* for the possibility of realising previous generation rights, because — without peace, a healthy environment and conditions of development — life, health, culture and the other demands referred to above are endangered.
2) These are rights which affect individuals, but through the protection of groups, whose peace, environment and development conditions may be endangered.
3) These rights quite clearly demand cooperation between national States and between the different Solidarity Organisations, because without this it proves absolutely impossible to protect them. They demand, as we shall see further on, co-responsibility.

Is it possible to protect these rights universally, taking into account that doing so is a requirement of justice?

4. Diligent reason as opposed to idle reason

In the *Fundamental Principles of the Metaphysics of Morals* Immanuel Kant affirmed that the awareness of the categorical imperative, of moral obligation, leads us to discover that we are free. "If I must act in a certain way, this is because I can do" — was Kant's reasoning. In the second half of the twentieth century German philosopher Hans Albert turned the already famous Kantian apothegm the other way round, converting this into an obvious "what cannot be done does not have to be done", a maxim to which he gave the name of "principle of realisability". Instead of advocating Utopias which invite one to do the unrealisable — what cannot be done — and which only cause frustration, injustice and disheartening in the long term, the principle of realisability reminds us that before affirming that something is obligatory, it is first necessary to find out if it is possible.

The principle of realisability is doubtlessly the result of overwhelming common sense, the problem being that it does not clear up who should decide what is realisable, which is extremely important. Because there are people who make use of a cruel and heartless *idle reason*, and see impossibilities everywhere, while others, led on by a *diligent reason*, which "appreciates, loves and considers from reflection", incredibly extend the sphere of what is possible. This is why I elsewhere proposed replacing Albert's maxim with another, considerably more diligent and realistic statement: *"what is necessary is possible and has to be made real"*.[29]

---

[29] A. Cortina, *Hasta un pueblo de demonios*, Introduction and chap. 1.

If, as has already been mentioned, it is already a *requirement of justice* today to protect those first three generations of rights which make the paradigmatic notion of social citizenship possible, the task of a diligent reason and will would consist in thinking out how to do it and put it into practice, not in seeking excuses alleging that it is impossible to protect them.[30] At least all the States that have ratified the 1948 Declaration would be committed to this task, and also all the people who know they are at the same time citizens of their own countries and citizens of the world.

However, if the rights of at least the first three generations belong to the type of rights whose satisfaction can be claimed in justice, and this is not a matter of charity, it would seem clear that all of these point to a notion of *recognition* between human beings, which would ultimately be the one that would give meaning to the contract.[31] This idea of recognition comes to the fore when we delve into what is the foundation of human rights and thus of the notion of social citizenship applied in advanced societies or at least in their Constitutions, if not in the actual situation.

5.   Pragmatic rights and human rights

This question of the possible foundation of human rights is doubtlessly a matter of great controversy in the philosophical world.[32] As far as I am concerned, in another work I argued in favour of a foundation for human rights based on the undeniable reality that human beings coordinate their lives by means of communicative action. This is a type of foundation which takes into account two sides of the phenomenon, transcendentality and history, and which thus transcends both substantialist iusnaturalism, which opts for particular unchanging rights, construed by authorised interpreters, and historicist legal positivism, anchored in particular historical will, unjust with the nature of the demands of reason, which go beyond particular historical contexts.[33]

As hermeneutics has shown, human reason is not a "pure reason" alien to history, uncontaminated by this, but *impure reason*, part of history and traditions.[34] But precisely this hermeneutics, if it is brave enough to be *critical*,

---

[30] See in this sense, for example A. Cortina (Ed.), *Construir confianza*, Madrid, Trotta, 2003.

[31] On this point see also G. González "En aras de la dignidad. Situación humana y moralidad", in ídem (coord.), *Derechos humanos. La condición humana en la sociedad tecnológica*, pp. 79-94.

[32] A.E. Pérez Luño, *Derechos humanos, Estado de derecho y Constitución*, chap. 3; J. Muguerza and other authors, *El fundamento de los derechos humanos*, Madrid, Debate, 1989.

[33] A. Cortina, *Ética sin moral*, Madrid, Tecnos, 1990, chap. 8.

[34] J. Conill, *El enigma del animal fantástico*, Madrid, Tecnos, 1991, especially part II.

discovers in historical experience — in this case that of communicative action — rational criteria allowing norms with a claim to universality to be formulated. In this case, they allow one to discover *demands* that, as conditions for a rational dialogue, must be satisfied and which I have called "pragmatic rights".

These rights are premises for discourse,[35] which leads Habermas and Alexy to affirm that they cannot pose any claim outside discourses, that is, in the sphere of action.[36] Nevertheless, if we remember that "pragmatic rights" are unavoidable premises for discourse, that practical discourse is the necessary extension of a communicative action, when one of its claims for rationality has been questioned (the claim to validity of the norm of action), and that communicative action is the mechanism for coordinating other human acts leading to ends, we have to conclude that pragmatic rights are premises of the rationality of any act with meaning. From this it ensues that the practice of discursive rationality in the practical sphere demands attention on two levels: the *transcendental level* of pragmatic rights, which have normative demands that have to be made concrete in the specific historical contexts of acts and the *historical level* of these contexts, in which the fundamental norms of morality and law have to be decided, taking into account concrete situations.

Pragmatic rights discover in turn a type of rights which could be qualified as "human", following the steps involved in the logic of practical discourse. Bearing in mind that a norm of action can only be considered correct if all those affected by it have been able to give their consent after a dialogue existing in ideal conditions of rationality,[37] the respect for a double type of rights would thus be inescapable:

1) The right to life of those affected by decisions of discourses, the right to participate in all the dialogues leading to decisions which affect them, the right to participate without coercion, the right to free expression, the right to be persuaded only by the power of the best argument, which demands not only freedom of conscience, religious freedom and freedom of opinion, but also freedom of association.

2) A type of rights without which the *télos* of discourse, which is agreement, would not be complied with, and whose configuration has to be historically

---

[35] For the ethics of discourse see, in Spain, A. Cortina, *Ética mínima*; *Ética sin moral*; *Ética aplicada y democracia radical*; J. Conill, *El enigma del animal fantástico*; J. Muguerza, *Desde la perplejidad*, Madrid, F.C.E., 1991; D. García-Marzá, *Ética de la justicia*, Madrid, Tecnos,1992; D. Blanco, J.A. Pérez Tapias and L. Sáez (eds.), *Discurso y realidad*, Madrid, Trotta, 1994, and monographic issue 183 of the magazine *Anthropos* (1999), on "Karl-Otto Apel. Una ética del discurso o dialógica".

[36] R. Alexy, *El concepto y la validez del derecho*, Barcelona, Gedisa, 1994,131-157.

[37] J. Habermas, *Faktizität und Geltung, Frankfurt, Suhrkamp*, pp. 109 and ff; *Wahrheit und Rechtfertigung*, Frankfurt, Suhrkamp, 1999.

specified; the right to material and cultural conditions allowing those affected to discuss and decide on an equal footing. The *télos* of language is the agreement, and it is impossible to *seriously* attempt to reach an agreement without attempting to give those who take part in the discussion a material and cultural standard of living allowing them to dialogue on an equal footing.

Any real consensus which decided to infringe any of the rights stated would go against the very premises by which the consensus had been reached, meaning that any decision thus made would be unjust. Hence the real consensus about specific human rights, which claim to be "legalised" in declarations and constitutions, must respect the ideally assumed rights and attempt to make these historically material, going by the particular circumstances in each case.

This process of making them material would take place in real, historically existing communities, through real consensuses, which always have to be reviewed and criticised from assumed rights, from the "cracks in Leviathan", which reveal the existence of a prior recognition, without which real contracts and consensuses lose their meaning and legitimacy. This is why it is important not to dry up the springs of recognition, but to let them flow in historically existing communities.

III. From individualism
to the political community

5. A JUST POLITICAL COMMUNITY

1. Neither individualism nor holism

Liberalism, as we have already been pointing out, was born in the West with the aim of defending individuals from outside interference, with the conviction that the individual is sacred for the individual, that he has an inalienable dignity, in virtue of which he possesses rights for whose protection the political community is created. From this perspective, the individual is "prior" to the political community, both ontologically and axiologically, meaning that the community is an instrument created for defending individual rights.

This form of thinking has been known as *"individualism"* as opposed to positions affirming the ontological and axiological priority of the group, of the social *"whole"* as opposed to individuals, positions which authors such as Louis Dumont group together under the heading of *"holism"*.[1] From this standpoint, individualism and holism would be two contrasting and irreconcilable patterns for conceiving social life. The contrast leaves holism in a very poor position, above all after the experiences of the Eastern countries, who had their civil societies and their pluralist life obliterated by the acts of a governing class which claimed to represent the will of the social whole. This is the reason why, in spite of the efforts of Hegel, Marx and Marxism in different versions, the post-liberal society in which we now live continues to opt for individualism against holism. It would be difficult to find a real justification of any other option, if indeed individualism and holism were the only alternatives.

But fortunately this is not the case. Fortunately, there are other options, apart from individualism and collectivist holism. First of all, because there are different varieties of individualism[2] which, from the standpoint of political philosophy, are embodied in a wide range of liberalisms: from the liberalism which rests on the theory of possessive individualism, going through the social liberalism of such authors as Rawls or Walzer, as far as liberalisms like the sort defended by Van Parijs in his *Real Freedom for All*, alleging that this is genuine liberalism, or the form defended by Amartya Sen in his capacities approach, so close to

---

[1] L. Dumont, *Essaies sur l'individualisme*, Paris, Ed. du Seuil, 1983. This is also similarly defended by G. Lipovetsky in *Le crépuscule du devoir*, Paris, Gallimard, 1992.

[2] S. Lukes, *Individualism*, Oxford, Blackwell, 1973; A. Renault, *L'ère de l'individu*, Paris, Gallimard, 1989.

the Marxist one of needs.[3] But secondly, because since ancient times there have been standpoints, often mixed up with the liberal ones just mentioned, taking either *the person with their social dimensions* as key for social interpretation, through understanding that the person is born of reciprocal recognition between human beings, or the *community of people*, through understanding that the person can only become independent in the community. These are rather differentiated positions, which continue to be valid today.

The second of these standpoints tends to claim that its origins lie in Aristotle and assures that in his *Politics* a road is opened up for conceiving social life that is perfectly usable today, though with some large-scale qualification. And though this standpoint is going to be discussed straight away, I should like to point out here and now that it does not stem so much from the texts in which Aristotle deals with democracy, either to criticise this as one of the deviant political systems, or to admit this as a lesser evil amongst the ingredients of the most sustainable political system, but in the texts in which Aristotle lays the foundations for a *politeia*, for a republic in agreement with the nature proper to it.

Legitimate regimes will be such precisely through having the common good as an aim, whilst deviant ones are such through having as an end the good of part of the society (one, a few, majority) but not that of society as a whole. Pursuing the common good, as is proper to *politeia*, requires virtue by citizens and civic friendship, both requisites which will be a more salient feature of the republican tradition than of democratic traditions.

These roots would seem to lead in our own times to the most promising communitarian movement, striving to link individual and community closely together, as well as republicanism in its different versions.

Kantian proposals of practical philosophy, as is the case of the ethics of discourse, and the hermeneutics of Ricoeur or Levinas, accentuate the side of reciprocal recognition between subjects rather than the communitarian one. Subjects are doubtlessly born in communities and they socialise and recognise each other as people in these, but precisely because each subject is able to recognise his or her identity with any human subject from any community, the limit for recognition is that of a universal community, which also includes future generations.

Communitarianism, republicanism and the *ethics of recognition* are located beyond individualism and holism, stressing the importance of the person and the community in a world which must necessarily have humanity as a whole as its horizon. We will have a brief look at these proposals and at their view of what a just community is.

---

[3] Ph. Van Parijs, *Real freedom for all*, Oxford, Clarendon Press, 1995; A. Sen, *Development as Freedom*; *Rationality and Freedom*, Harvard Univ. Press, 2002.

2. From rights to strong evaluations

To affirm the priority of the individual and the individual's rights with certain liberals leaves a number of questions open, such as the following: Why is the recognition of moral demands, to which we referred in the previous section, a symptom of "civilisation"? What authorises the countries which have ratified the 1948 Declaration to lay down what is "civilised" and what is not?

It is in this respect that an author such as Charles Taylor reminds us that in spite of all liberals' insistence on affirming the social predominance of the individual and the individual's rights, what instead occurs actually is that certain *capacities*, which seem essential to us culturally to lead a human life, make us feel obliged to protect these, to clothe them, and then put them forward as *rights*.

But the *evaluation* of these capacities is cultural — it is a culture which appreciates certain capacities (those of expressing oneself freely, fashioning one's own opinion, having a private property ownership system, etc.) — in such a way that it considers practising these to be a *requirement*, essential for realising humanity itself in fullness. Other cultures do not see this matter the same way, which is why it ensues that, in spite of liberal attempts to prioritise rights, the *evaluations* of these capacities are more original than rights.[4]

Taylor's affirmations have encountered certain replies retorting that universalism defending human rights is not proper only to western culture, but also to eastern cultures, such as Buddhism, in which tolerance has a longer history than in the west. Nevertheless, though it may be right insofar as an eastern claim to universalism goes, this criticism does not affect Taylor's argument, for at least two reasons.

First of all, because Taylor is right in asserting that it is in specific communities that we have learned to value exercising particular capacities to such a point that it proves difficult to us to accept that it is possible to be a full person without doing so, and we understand that these communities have the duty of justice to propitiate such capacities, because it is also within their power. The claim to universality of judgements about what is just may well be formally present in all cultures, but what is indeed true is that, as regards specific contents, not all cultures understand that expressing one's own opinion, forming one's own conscience, moving round freely, etc., are capacities whose practice proves essential.

Secondly, it is also true that it is formal Western ethics which have expressed the formal claim to universality of judgements on what is just in philosophical

---

[4] Ch. Taylor, "Atomism", in *Philosophy and the Human Sciences: Philosophical Papers*, II, 1985, pp. 187-210.

language, displaying in concepts that it is important to reach a match between form and content. This is a point that we shall deal with in Chapter 8, when considering the possibilities of a global ethics. For the time being, we return to Taylor's argument, to which Amartya Sen also subscribes to some extent when proposing *reasoned evaluation* as a method for elucidating what the order of the people's functions should be when making these possible socially, to avoid substantial inequalities and serious injustice.[5] Unlike Martha Nussbaum, who gives a list of capacities whose practice is vital to lead a thriving life, Sen appeals to public deliberation and to reasoned valuation to discern the order in which societies should cope with their members' functions.[6] However, might the evaluations that interlocutors have assumed in their community through the socialisation process perhaps not guide a reasoned valuation, a deliberation which attempts to reach a consensus?

If this is the case, if there is no "axiologically neutral" defence of rights, but if the defence of concrete rights instead depends on socially learned "strong evaluations", liberalism is not self-sufficient, but refers us to communities in which these capacities are valued, and ultimately refers us to the specific communities in which human beings learn to assess.

3. Community by nature

In Book I of *Politics* Aristotle points out that the human being is by nature a social animal and that, also by nature, one that forms part of different communities (family, ethnic group) existing within a political community, which is the one that precedes all the others. Unlike the position that Hobbes would defend centuries later, that the political community is constituted artificially, Aristotle would say that man is naturally social and forms part of a political community also by nature, and not by contrivance.

The reason why man is a social animal is as follows: nature does nothing in vain and man is the only animal endowed with the word, and not only a voice: the voice is a sign of pain and pleasure, which is why other animals also have one, but the word is for stating what is advisable and what is harmful, what is just and what unjust, and only man has the sense of right and wrong, of what is just and what unjust. The place in which human beings jointly debate to determine what is just and what unjust is the city, the *polis*, the political community.[7]

---

[5] A.K. Sen, "From Income Inequality to Economic Inequality", in *Southern Economic Journal*, 64, 2 (1997), pp. 397 and 398.

[6] D.A. Crocker, "Functioning and Capability. The Foundations of Sen's and Nussbaum's Development Ethic", in *Political Theory*, vol. 20, n. 4 (1992), pp. 584-612.

[7] Aristotle, *Politics*, I, 1, 1253 to 7-18.

The political community is characterised by being self-sufficient, while other forms of community, such as the family or the ethnic group, have to live within the political community, because they cannot survive outside this. One should at this point make it clear that the republican tradition does not identify the ethnic community with political community, but that the political community is characterised by making coexistence of different families and different ethnic groups possible, something into which modern liberalism will only go more deeply. This is why ethnic nationalism is not backed by any of the traditions of political philosophy which set out to explain the political order by appealing, not to irrational and thus inhuman sentiments, but to rational feelings, or, the same thing, sentient reason.[8] The human being — Aristotle said — is "desiring intellect" or "thinking desire", and this is also true for political life. Hence a political community founded only on the feeling of belonging will be unable to incorporate this basic feeling of political life, which is the rational sentiment of justice. One can argue about what is just, what is just is also the subject of public deliberation.

As regards the individuals who form part of the political community, Aristotle understands that the whole is prior to the part, in the sense that the satisfaction of the individual's interests depends to a large extent on the satisfaction of the community's interests. If the latter fails to thrive, it will be difficult for individuals to be able to be happy, as the welfare of the community propitiates that of individuals. The idea of individual, the conviction that there may be a contrast between the individual's interests and those of the community, is a modern idea; to such an extent that Modernity has on occasions been characterised as the "Age of the Individual".[9]

However, what is the backbone of the community? What is the order of the community? The reply to this question is clear; order is justice, disorder, injustice. As we have already stated, the political community is thus not only the place of belonging, but also the society which seeks to structure itself fairly and which has to have at least two ingredients, *friendship* between citizens, understood as concord, and *civic virtue*.

Unlike the anatomy and the physiology of the political body that Hobbes outlined at the beginning of *Leviathan*, in the political body that Aristotle designed at the beginning of his *Politics,* friendship, concord, keeps communities bonded together, while discord separates them. "When men are friends — Aristotle would say expressly — there is no need for justice, but even while being just they also require friendship, and it would seem that it is the just who

---

[8] A. Cortina, "Reflexiones éticas en torno al nacionalismo", in *Sal Terrae*, 1.023 (1999), pp. 381-392.

[9] A. Renaut, *L'ère de l'individu*, Paris, Gallimard, 1989.

are more capable of friendship".[10] And on the other hand, in the absence of citizens with deeply rooted virtue the city breaks down, because it lives from the virtue of its members.

This is why in my opinion, the central matter in the structure of modern practical reason is not so much "Israel or Athens",[11] a question which in our book becomes "Covenant or Republic". The central question, since the structure of politics, ethics and religion depends on this, would seem instead to be in theory *"Covenant, Republic or Contract"* — "Israel, Athens or London" — because contractualism is the mark of modern politics, while the Covenant is, as we shall see, a premise of the contract.

It might also be the case that the three narrations, that of *Genesis*, Aristotle's *Politics* and the *Leviathan* are now so very mingled that it is impossible to separate them. That "fusion of horizons" which Gadamer so perceptively talks about would have occurred, and the question would then be to start philosophically designing the most appropriate articulation. We will thus continue for the time being with two tales which entwine *prima facie* in the justification of the modern political community, that of the republic and that of the contract.

4. Republic or contract?

The Aristotelian political community indeed lacks what we would today consider to be clear limits, since as has been said time and time again, it does not consider all its members as being citizens, but only those who have certain characteristics, and understands that Athenian citizens are free men, but not all human beings are free. The universalist principle of post-conventional morality is not to be found here, this being instead a *conventional communitarianism* which has still not assumed the universalisation of freedom, nor that such freedom is understood as being autonomy.[12]

What matters is the *êthos* of the community, the character of the community, in which citizens jointly deliberate on what is just and what unjust, and rooted in this notion of politics are different traditions which in our times vie to display their differential nature.

We could for example mention the *republican traditions* of different sorts which would have at least the following common traits:[13] 1) Man is by nature

---

[10] Aristotle, *Nicomachean Ethics*, VIII, 1, 1155 to 26-28.

[11] J. Habermas, *Vom sinnlichen Eindruck zum symbolischen Ausdrucks*, Frankfurt, Suhrkamp, 1997.

[12] J. Conill, "Ideologías políticas", in A. Cortina (dir.), *Diez palabras clave en filosofía política*, pp. 213-258.

[13] R. Dahl, *Democracy and its critics*, New Haven, Yale University Press, 1989, chap. 2.

a social and political animal, who should live in political association if he intends to develop all his potentialities. 2) A good man should be a good citizen. 3) A good political system is an association consisting of good citizens. 4) A good political system reflects and promotes its members' virtue. 5) The best political system is one in which citizens are equal before the law. 6) A political system which does not involve the participation of its citizens cannot be legitimate. 7) Since there are different factions and classes amongst the people, a constitution reflecting the interests of the different groups has to be drawn up.

However, these common denominators do not mean that there is not a wide range of republicanisms, and it is very hard today to locate the republican traditions on the map of tendencies of political philosophy. We shall look at three illustrations in this respect: that of Habermas in "Three normative models of democracy", that of Philip Pettit in *Republicanism* and that of Rawls in *Political Liberalism*.[14]

Habermas distinguishes between a communitarian-republican model, like Michelman's, a classical liberal model, and a third model, that of a deliberative democracy, which politically embodies the Principle of Discourse.

In the communitarian-republican model, the community is the core of political life, the force of communicative power is a political force, law is objective law and there is a certain identification between political life and ethical life, between common good and morality. If in the distinction between moral, ethical and pragmatic reasons, some have more weight than others in this model, these would be the ethical ones, the ones backed by the *êthos* of the political community, in what Hegel understands as "*Sittlichkeit*".

In the liberal model of democracy the individual is the nucleus of shared life, the political process is an instrument for balancing individual interests, it is important to defend citizens' subjective rights and the reasons which sustain legal norms are very particularly pragmatic.

Lastly, as far as deliberative democracy is concerned, the key item of the political apparatus is intersubjectivity, reciprocal recognition of subjects, which is expressed in the systems of language and founds the communicative power by means of which political power is legitimated. At this point, that of recognising the force of communicative power, deliberative democracy ties in with republicanism. But it disagrees with it through considering the distinction between "*Moralität*" and "*Sittlichkeit*" as being necessary: the reasons for supporting the validity of legal norms are not basically ethical (stemming from the substantive conception of the community's good), but also pragmatic, as liberals wish, and also moral. The substantive conception of the good of the political

---

[14] J. Habermas, "Drei normative Demokratiemodelle", in *Die Einbeziehung des Anderen*, chap. 7; P. Pettit, *Republicanism*, Oxford, Oxford University Press, 1997.

community has to be measured by moral principles of justice, which include the republic of all human beings. As can easily be seen, on the Habermasian map republicanism is aligned with communitarianism, leaving liberalism at the opposite end of the scale.

Pettit, however, proposes a different map. For him communitarianism would be located at one pole, adducing a substantive conception of good for the political community; liberalism would be at the opposite pole, defending above all basic liberties, that is, liberties which come under the heading of "non-interference", and republicanism, lastly, would be located between communitarianism and liberalism, taking freedom understood as "non-domination" as its watchword. But it is not just a matter of republicanism not being identified with communitarianism, as this would actually be closer to liberalism than to communitarianism, to such an extent that we could in fact talk of a "liberal republicanism". As Jesús Conill points out, the distinctive element between the different political conceptions is the form of conceiving freedom, the concept of freedom.[15]

Nevertheless, the question becomes more complicated if we go by the *Rawlsian* distinction between two traditions that are actually republican, *"classical republicanism"* and *"civic humanism"*, and by the way he locates his political liberalism in relation to these.

Rawls says: "I understand by classical republicanism the standpoint according to which, if the citizens of a democratic society wish to preserve their basic rights and freedoms (including civil liberties guaranteeing the freedoms of private life) they should also have the 'political virtues' (as I called them) to a sufficient extent and be willing to take part in public life".[16] From this angle, one is not proposing citizens' participation in public life as the model of happy life that they should include, but as a means for defending democratic liberties. A healthy democracy requires a degree of citizens' participation, quite aside from whether some citizens see the model of a life worthy of being lived in the practice of such participation.

This brings to mind echoes of the talk by Constant, unquestionably liberal, entitled "On the freedom of the Ancients compared with that of the Moderns" in the final section in which the author advises us not to replace the freedom of the modern (understood as independence) with the freedom of the ancients (understood as participation in the *res publica*), but to give priority to that of the moderns, taking participation in citizens' lives as a means for defending that independence. If citizens become accustomed to reclusion in private life,

---

[15] J. Conill, D. Crocker (Eds.), *Republicamismo y Educación Cívica*, Granada, Comares, 2003.
[16] J. Rawls, *Political Liberalism*, New York, Columbia University Press, 1993, p. 205.

public powers may deprive them even of that range of basic freedoms which form the freedom of the modern. Participation is thus not *the* happiness-making way of life, but a means for defending basic freedoms.

In this tradition Rawls includes the Machiavelli of the *Discourses*, but above all *Democracy in America* by Alexis de Tocqueville, and explains that his political liberalism does not disagree with this classical republicanism, to the extent that it does not propose a model of happy life for the public realm, which is indeed done in his opinion by "civic humanism".

Following Taylor, Rawls understands "civic humanism" as being a variant of Aristotelianism, a doctrine by which man fulfils his essential nature to the fullest extent in a democratic society, in whose life there is broad and vigorous participation. Participation is not a necessary condition for the protection of basic freedoms, but the exceptional sphere of good life. Rousseau would be the most perfected example of this humanity, and Hannah Arendt an excellent contemporary representative. Political liberalism cannot trade with civic humanism thus understood, because this proposes a comprehensive doctrine of good, which I would call an "ethics of maxima", in which participation is an essential ingredient.

Nevertheless, the denominations used by Rawls are actually as questionable as any others. First of all because, as far as I know, no republican tradition excludes Rousseau from its party, and as regards Hannah Arendt, the most fruitful part of her contribution consists in defending that "political power" is the capacity to act in an organised way, meaning that the relations of political power are the relations of *isonomy*, the relations between equals befitting the republic, from which one reaches mutual consent. Authority is not linked to domination, but to the recognition obtained by whomsoever deserves this, which is why violence and persuasion are ruled out. And just as there is no politics without power characterised in this way — Arendt believes —, neither is there politics with violence; violence, as an instrument for obtaining obedience, belongs to the prepolitical stage, while politics strictly speaking starts with the dialogue and instauration of freedoms. In fact Habermas himself, who is anything but a perfectionist, recognised the debt of his deliberative democracy to Arendt's republicanism.[17]

Apart from this, the traditions coming under the "civic humanism" banner repeatedly appeal to Tocqueville. Indeed, Tocqueville tackles what continues to be the radical question of political philosophy and social science early this century, "how to build a firmly established democracy, able to do justice to human beings' equal aspiration to liberty?", and to reply to this he outlines a civic humanism, opposed to apathetic individualism, which is responsible for democratic anaemia. As Juan Manuel Ros rightly points out, there are three keys to

---

[17] J. Habermas, *Philosophisch-politische Profile*, Frankfurt, Suhrkamp, 1971.

Tocqueville's thought which are extremely fruitful for the present times: the critique of democratic individualism and the proposal for a committed civic humanism, the dialectic of freedom and equality, and the necessary connection between democracy and civil society.[18]

Having thus shown that the labels of "classical republicanism" and "civic humanism" do not prove to be excessively useful, it would be advisable to go the root of the question before locating the different traditions in the atlas of political philosophy and before giving these names. The heart of the matter would, according to Rawls, be this: some republican traditions consider that a life "worthy of being lived", a happy life, is the one lived by a citizen in a political community, meaning that there is no difference between what is just and what is good, but that what is good is obtained in the polis, while other republican traditions come closer to the liberal model, and consider that the political sphere should ensure justice in shared life, and that achieving a just community demands citizens' participation, but without making participation a way of life.

In my opinion, the first case is actually a *"perfectionist republicanism"* which designs a model of man and his development in social life, a "perfectionist" ethics which points out some characteristics as being essentially human and understands that these are the ones that a State should reinforce. In the second case we would be in the sphere of a *"liberal republicanism"*, which does not set out to design a model of man, but only to show what political life should be like to allow the development of freedoms. This last model would include as I see it most of today's republican proposals, whilst perfectionist republicanism would come closer to communitarianism.

5. Liberal republicanism

Liberal republicanism, advocated nowadays by a large number of authors, such as Barber, Dworkin, Pettit or Renaut, puts forward a pattern of political community in which republic and contract are actually entwined. Although each of these authors makes his own specific proposal, perhaps the one best embracing the others, with a specifically republican flavour at the same time, is that of Philip Pettit in *Republicanism*.

Indeed, Pettit insists that the central notion of republican political life must be freedom, understood as non-domination, and from this point he understands that a community is free when the structure of the institutions is such that none

---

[18] J.M. Ros, *Los dilemas de la democracia liberal. Sociedad civil y democracia en Tocqueville*, Barcelona, Crítica, 2001.

of its members fear any arbitrary interference in their lives from the powerful, depending on their state of mind or mood, nor need to ingratiate themselves with them to get their due in justice, but instead that all can look each other in the eye on an equal footing, since servility is not required.[19] This does not mean that decisions are taken in assemblies, nor that all the members of the group continuously participate in decisions of shared life, but that all members know what they are liable to and do not feel forced to strategically defend themselves from the ambitious, to be alert to their changes in mood nor resort to false praise to enjoy security.

In a genuine republican community the *laws* are an expression of freedom, and not weapons in the hands of feudal despots to help their vassals and crush any who do not bend their knee; *civic virtue* combines the aspirations of those who have the same aim and backs the laws desired by them; public decisions are taken through common *deliberation*, which leads to determining what is just, and not from negotiations and agreements which are always detrimental to the weakest, those who have to be satisfied with little so as not to lose it all; the *social capital* of shared ethical values provides common ground. These would be the traits of a *republican tradition*, which ought to be incorporated by the public institutions of a democratic society to gradually generate an "intangible hand", able to transform particular preferences into common targets. Not the *invisible* hand, presumably harmonising conflicting preferences, but the *intangible* hand of common convictions, which congregates individuals behind the same public proposal.

Is this liberal republicanism so far from communitarianism? Can it really be said that the communitarian movement comes close to perfectionist republicanism, which understands that the model of worthy life is participation in the community?

I am afraid that ultimately modern communitarians and liberal republicans end up converging very closely and insisting above all on fostering two types of social capital; that of democratic values, which constitute the common ground from which it is possible to really build the political community, and that of civil society associations, without which there is no genuine democracy and not even the economy works.

6.   The community, between the individual and the State

Present communitarianism ties in with Aristotle's republican tradition and also takes from Hegel the conviction that morality has to be embodied in the institutions and customs of concrete communities. This is why, like Hegel, it is

---

[19] Ph. Pettit, *Republicanism*, pp. 22, 44-46; P. Savidan, "La crítica republicana del liberalismo", en J. Conill y D. Crocker, 135-158.

opposed to present-day contractualisms, understanding that liberal contractualism starts from at least four abstractions:

1) Understanding that *the "self" is a rational individual*, who chooses his or her form of life from plans and projects, when most of the relations undertaken are actually not so "freely" chosen, but to a great extent conditioned, such as one's companion or career, and when their identity is in reality closely linked to non-chosen communities.

2) *Formal universalism*, to the extent that the liberal ends up losing all sensitivity for context. It is in fact better to interpret meanings already shared for our communities.

3) *Priority of the individual and his or her rights*, which are actually highly valued capacities in a community, which is why it would be better for the citizen to also assume the responsibility for that community, lest those capacities should cease to be values and the demanding nature of rights should be watered down.

4) The *voice of the conscience* seems sufficient to keep guard over morality. But this is not the case: morality is to a very large extent a matter of the community. This is why the conversion of the heart, to which Kant resorted, is not enough, but why it is also necessary to renew social bonds and reform public life.

From this criticism, which obviously, as will be shown below, goes along with a positive orientation for action, the social axis of the new paradigm is the community, located between the individual and the State. This could mean a certain return to Aristotelianism, but authors such as Etzioni or Barber nevertheless make it increasingly clear that this is no solution, it being instead a question of realising that personal freedom can only be conquered in the community. Not only should the community not stifle the individual, but it is also the condition for allowing their autonomy.[20] But at the same time the realisation of autonomy in the community demands that the individual should be responsible for his community, give this loyalty and be in this sense a "patriot".[21] This is why the New Golden Rule, which should govern relations between individuals and the community is: "respect and defend the moral order of society in the same way as you would like society to respect and defend your autonomy".[22]

In this sense the task of moral education is vital in a society, a basic necessity product, because the laws are important in a social setting, but the moral

---

[20] B. Barber, *Strong Democracy*, Berkeley/Los Angeles/London, University of California Press, 1984.

[21] On the patriotism-cosmopolitism controversy see chap. 8 of this book.

[22] A. Etzioni, *The New Golden Rule*, New York, Basic Books, Preface.

commitments taken on by its members are even more so. The laws are essential, but customs are even more so, as Tocqueville already pointed out. Morally educating people, through the school and in the structure of civil society, proves urgent for any society wishing to be really free and democratic.

Nevertheless, the difficulties start when attempting to clarify what type of community we are referring to, because if this is an intermediary between the individual and the State, if it consists of these networks of civil society associations able to educate in pluralism without coercion, then this is no longer identified simply with the political community. The State has a subsidiary function here, and has to do what associations on a local sphere (family, school, municipality) are not able to do; and what is actually being done is to attempt to create and further social capital, the system of associations which creates links between people.

Indeed, Etzioni assures that we are not using the "community" to refer to only one of these, but to the individual's necessity to become independent within a set of communities, which act like those sets of Matrioska dolls or Chinese boxes (families, neighbouring communities, religious communities, professional associations and labour associations, peoples, cities, national communities and transnational communities). The result of this ensemble will be a *community of communities*, constituted by the relationship between communities which keep their cultural particularities, but with a common commitment. This community of communities — Etzioni would say- is represented as a *mosaic* and has a *substantive nucleus of shared values*, not only procedural values and the formal mechanisms of democracy, because this substantive nucleus actually proves to be essential to maintain social order.[23]

Nevertheless, when attempting to determine what values these are, we realise that "substantialist" ethics are closer than they appear to "proceduralist" ethics; we see that the Hegelians are closer to Kantians than might appear at first glance,[24] because these values are as follows: the commitment to democracy, respect for difference, encouraging dialogues open to society, fostering the means required to reconcile individuals who have harmed the community.

Are these ethical values which today distinguish some political communities from others, meaning that we can say that some communities defend these values and others do not?

The question is not a minor one, because in the controversy between universalists and communitarians the latter are supposed to defend the standpoint of the *êthos* of specific communities, whilst the universalists defend what has been called the "moral standpoint", which is that of impartiality. If this were

---

[23] A. Etzioni, "The Community of Communities", in *The Responsive Community*, 7(1996/97), pp. 21-32.
[24] A. Cortina, *Ética sin moral*, chap. 2.

the case, the *êthos*, the characteristic nature of each community, would have to contain some value or some values which distinguish it from others, which is why those who wish to defend those values should also assume responsibility for the community so that this can go on teaching these.

But the point is that the values that we have mentioned are from Etzioni's viewpoint common today to at least all societies with a liberal democracy. None of these would dare to say that it does not appreciate as positive values the commitment to democracy, the respect for difference or dialogue, and many other values that are today at least verbally defended by Western culture and which are today being "globalised", also at least verbally.

Although we can distinguish, with Habermas, between pragmatic reasons for justifying moral standards (those of convenience in a particular situation), ethical reasons (backed by history and traditions which mark the character of a specific political community) and moral reasons (the ones which come into play when we take humanity as a whole into account), the values that we have mentioned would not seem to be able to belong to the "*ethical*" sphere of one community as compared with all the rest. It seems instead that we have referred to *moral values*, today common to the *êthos* of a large number of political communities, communities which would seem to be distinguished from one another by consuetudinary rather than moral traits.

This is where we would find the famous "constitutional patriotism", which in my opinion is not what distinguishes some political communities from others, since practically all countries with liberal democracy defend the same constitutional values.[25]

One could thus think that today's communitarianism does not identify the political community with the moral community, but instead sets out to further associations in civil society, because it trusts in these as conveyors of moral values; above all, the associations of a more traditional kind. Being responsible for specific communities is important, not because they defend values that no-one else defends (something which is clearly false), but because the commitment to the local sphere is essential to realise the universal one, too. Losing interest for what is nearest, for the community to which one belongs, is not the best way to construct a republic of all humanity, quite the opposite indeed, but at the same time the moral horizon of specific political communities can only be that of humanity as a whole.

Perhaps it is here that the essential difference between enlightened communitarianism and liberal republicanism lies: in the type of associations which they set out to foster; more traditional ones in the first case, including those in

---

[25] J. Habermas, *Die Einbeziehung des Anderen*, above all Part II.

which individuals maintain hierarchical relations with each other, and horizontal relations in the second case. But in any event, both indicate the need for strengthening social capital.

6. SOCIAL CAPITAL: THE WEALTH OF NATIONS

1. Circles are not squares

In their public statements the United Nations and western societies tend to claim the quadrature of the circle. On one hand, they foster individualist culture, in which, as Hegel said — "each person is an end for himself and others are nothing for him". But they then go straight on to request solidarity with the weak and vulnerable, because this is what verbally legitimates the institutions of the western world, acting as mouthpieces for defence of human rights, arranging summit conferences, congresses, conferences on poverty and exclusion, and ending up verbally agreeing that Rawls is right when he says that a system is just if it benefits the least well-off in society more than any other possible arrangement. It is indeed a gruelling task to link individualism and presumed solidarity, tantamount to squaring a circle.

But circles are round, not square. Solidarity and justice do not emerge from a world in which each is an end for himself and others are nothing for him. That is why it is important to propose designs of round circles, to sketch out the outlines of a society in which the elementary minima of justice, without which a society can hardly call itself human, can thrive. And in such a design an important role will be taken by the unrenounceable cultivation of *social capital*, wealth which places us beyond selfish individualism and undesirable collectivism.

The concept of social capital is again brought up for consideration through the work by Robert D. Putnam, *Making Democracy Work: Civic Traditions in Modern Italy*, published in 1993. According to the author himself, the book is the result of an almost experimental study on subnational governments in the different regions in Italy lasting twenty years, undertaken with the aim of finding out what it is that makes democratic governments govern efficiently in certain regions, whilst in others the degree of efficiency is very low. Instead of criticising the political, economic and social institutions of certain countries, Putnam understands on good grounds that it proves more advisable to study the reasons why democracy works better in certain places than others and to learn from the former.

The conclusion drawn by Putnam is extremely thought-provoking, although it is not sufficiently backed from the empirical standpoint: the quality of representative governments is determined by the presence of extended traditions of civic commitment or by the lack of these. The difference between the regions in the north of Italy and the southern ones is due to the fact that in the former there is a long tradition of networks of civic commitment and reciprocity which is lacking in the south. This means that there is a relationship between the performance of institutions and the power and density of civil society, between the operation of democratic governments and the associative capacity of the members of civil society.

And what is more, there is even a relationship between these civic commitment networks and the good running of the economy. Historical analysis suggests that organised reciprocity and civic solidarity networks constitute a precondition of socio-economic modernisation, that is, of proper operation of democracy and the economy. In this line of work, or approaches close to this, some social scientists propose a common structure for understanding mechanisms through which results such as more effective governments or faster economic development are produced. The name given to this structure is "social capital".

The same Francis Fukuyama, in books such as *Trust* and *The Great Disruption*, recognises that the stability and prosperity of post-industrial societies demand habits of reciprocity and confidence: believing that the desire for profit is the only ingredient of the modern economy implies not having understood Adam Smith at all and reducing his economic and moral work to the famous text about the baker, the brewer and the butcher. Without a doubt the desire for profit is a motive for trade, but Smith himself is very aware of the fact that there are other motives, and above all, that the economic process does not come down to trade, but also involves production and distribution; these being states that, to function properly, require institutions, laws and other habits of reciprocity and trust that constitute the moral fabric of a society.[26] This fabric has been vaguely called "social capital".

When the story of the notion of "social capital" is being told, it tends to be said that it was Lyda Judson Hanifan who first used the expression, in 1916, to describe rural community schools. According to Putnam, the first female scholar to use the term "social capital" is Jane Jacobs in *The Death and Life of Great American Cities* (1961) to refer to the social networks found in certain urban districts, whose existence favoured public security. But there is actually widespread agreement in attributing the authorship of the notion, though not the term, of social capital to Alexis de Tocqueville.

In his trip to America in 1830 Tocqueville appreciated one of the greatest differences between the United States and the French as consisting in the propensity of the former to practise the *"associative art"*. He asserted that

---

[26] A. Sen, "Does Business Ethics Make Economic Sense?", in *Business Ethics Quarterly*, vol. 3, issue 1 (1993), pp. 45-54; J. Conill, "De Adam Smith al 'imperialismo económico'", in *Claves de razón práctica*, 66 (1996), pp. 52-56.

"Nothing is more deserving of attention than the intellectual and moral associations in America". It is precisely this capacity to form associations of all kinds that enables solutions avoiding two equally undesirable extremes: individualism and collectivism, the latter also in its state-run version; but at the same time this inclination of Americans towards civic association can in turn be understood as a key to their unprecedented skill in making democracy work. This associative wealth was what allowed democracy to work better in America than in France, by furthering the central role of civil society in the organisation of life.

Taking the peculiar notion of "heart" from Pascal, Tocqueville saw on his trip to America that peoples' *habits of heart* are more important for embodying democracy than laws, and laws more important than the geographical constitution, as Robert Bellah pointed out a few years ago in *Habits of the heart*.[27]

Going on in Tocqueville's wake, recent sociologists attempt to empirically show that the quality of public life and the action of social institutions are influenced by standards and networks of civic commitment. And on the other hand, they also make an effort to show with empirical data that the role of social networks is crucial in the economic sphere, not only in the "developing" countries, but also in the developed countries and in the "network capitalism" of eastern Asia. Curiously, these interpersonal and interorganisational systems surround ultra-modern industries, from Silicon Valley to Benetton.

2.   Eradicating anomy

Nevertheless, North American associative wealth seems to have considerable waned over recent times, as shown, amongst others, by Fukuyama in *The Great Disruption* and Putnam himself, in an emblematic article in 1995, which to some extent reconsidered his previous position and has received at least as much criticism as *To make democracy work*, criticisms to which the author has gradually responded: this article is "Bowling Alone: America's Declining Social Capital".[28]

The metaphor is extremely thought-provoking. Between 1980 and 1993 numbers of bowls players increased by 10% in the United States, while the leagues

---

[27] R.N. Bellah et alii, *Habits of the Heart*, Berkeley, University of California Press, 1985, chap. 2.

[28] R.D. Putnam, "Bowling Alone: America's Declining Social Capital", *Journal of Democracy*, 6 (1995), pp. 65-78; "Bowling Alone Revisited", in *Responsive Community*, 5 (1995), pp. 18-33; "The Strange Disappearance of Civic America", in *American Prospect*, 24 (1996), pp. 34-48; *Bowling Alone*, 2002.

of bowls players dropped by 40%. The owners of bowling alleys complain because their income came more from the beer and pizzas consumed by members of players' leagues than the rental of bowls, and solitary players prove to consume at least three times less than those who play in company.

It is plain to see that the case of bowls players is more a metaphor than a piece of empirical proof. It is a matter of detecting how civic commitment networks have greatly declined since the seventies. Fewer people vote, and there has been a drop in religious affiliation and membership of trade unions, associations of parents and teachers, civic organisations. The associations still thriving are more the sort with members who pay a quota than those of people who relate with one another. It is true that there are new forms of association, such as those of the ecologists or feminists, but Putnam considers that they do not create networks of trust, but are instead "tertiary" organisations. And as regards Third Sector associations, which have grown over recent times, Putnam understands that these do not always create networks of trust.

However, this chapter does not aim to deal with the criticism that Putnam's work has met, nor his replies to this, seeking instead to point out a concern which is not only Putnam's, but also shared by a large number of authors in our present times. In advanced countries anomy, which was detected so lucidly by Durkheim, is a profound ill affecting the social body. Individuals do not identify themselves with the laws and values of their society, because they have doubts about enjoying reciprocity in the event of committing themselves to these and do not believe that their institutions are going to respond fittingly. Such authors as Bellah, MacIntyre and Sandel indicate the same danger, against which one should only intensify associative networks and the expectations of reciprocity. The only way out of this is to further social capital.

3. The imperialism of economic rationality

Some social scientists have in recent times suggested a common structure for understanding the mechanisms by means of which results such as more effective government, faster economic development, etc. are achieved, and give this the name of "social capital". Nevertheless, the merit for having developed the theoretical framework of social capital for the first time has unquestionably been attributed to James S. Coleman.[29] Coleman's intuition is extremely thought-provoking, with the observation that two broad intellectual currents can be seen in any description and explanation of social action.

---

[29] J.S. Coleman, "Social Capital in the Creation of Human Capital", *AJS*, vol. 94 Supplement (1988), pp. 95-120.

One of these, proper to the work of many sociologists, is characterised by considering the actor as socialised, as being governed by social norms. It involves the advantage of dealing with this undeniable aspect of personal life, which is the enormous influence of the socialisation process and social norms on the person, but also has a serious disadvantage, which is that of not pointing out an "engine of action". The actor is moulded by the environment, but the internal engines of action, which are what give it a purpose or direction, are not shown.

The *other intellectual current* is proper to the work of many economists. It considers the actor as having objectives which he or she reaches independently, as a party interested in maximising their utility. This is a trend found in the neo-classical economy and also in currents of political philosophy, such as utilitarianism, contractualism and certain theories of natural rights. "Economic imperialism in epistemology" proves undeniable.

Nonetheless, this economicist, rather than economic, trend also has a serious flaw, which is that it reveals a motive for action (maximisation of utility) but neglects the essential aspect stressed by sociologists, which is that people's actions are fashioned by the social context. Social organisation is essential in the operation, not only of society, but also of the economy.

Coleman's objective thus consists in importing the principle of rational action to use this in the analysis of the social system, including the economic system, but not limiting itself to this, and doing so without discarding social organisation in the process. In this context, the concept of social capital is an instrument of assistance, because if we take the theory of rational action (in which each actor has control over certain resources and interest in certain resources) as starting point, social capital constitutes a particular type of the actor's resources. Social capital consists of certain aspects of social structure, facilitating certain action by the actors.

At this point Coleman avails himself of the extension of the concept of capital proposed by Gary Becker[30] and adds a third form, social capital. The three forms of capital, physical, human and social, facilitate production work: 1) *Physical capital* — consisting of land, buildings, machines, earth — is created by changes to construct tools facilitating production; 2) *Human capital*, consisting of the techniques and knowledge available to a company or society, which has been known as "human resources", is created by means of changes in persons, producing skills and capacities which allow them to act in new ways; 3) *Social capital*, nevertheless, is produced by changes in relationships between people, changes which facilitate action. It is not located in physical objects, it is not tangible like physical capital, but is instead *intangible*, like

---

[30] G. Becker, *Human Capital*, New York, National Bureau of Economic Research, 1964.

human capital. But, we could say, it is even "less tangible" than human capital, because it exists in relations between persons and not in persons themselves. Locating social capital in relationships between persons, even though this implies persons, and not in persons themselves, is one of the features of Coleman's conception.

Social capital is thus a resource for people and organisations, in the same way as physical and human capitals are, and to such an extent that some social scientists assert that national economies depend on at least these three forms of capital.[31] And as has already been mentioned in previous chapters, both theorists of republicanism and those of communitarianism propose increasing social capital. Is this only a resource for accomplishing certain objectives, or is it something also valuable in itself?

4. Social capital is a public asset

Coleman points out three essential forms of social capital. The first refers to the *obligations, expectations and reliability* of social structures, which act as credits for others' (persons or corporate actors) action, in an analogy with financial capital. In some social structures people are already doing things for other persons, there thus being many "credit vouchers". In other social structures there are fewer, because individuals are more self-sufficient.

This form of social capital depends on the reliability of the social environment (obligations have to be returned) and on the current extension of the obligations that it maintains. All these matters have their light and dark sides, because at first sight it would seem that a wider network of credit relations is superior to a smaller one, but one should nevertheless remember that in a society individuals differ from one another in the number of credits and the person who has most is not the most altruistic, but instead the godfather.

Another important form of social capital is the *potential for information* inherent to social relations. Information is an important base for action, obtained by persons who are involved in social networks.

A third form of social capital would be *effective norms and penalties*. It is unlikely for societies presided over by anomy to propose joint objectives, because their members cannot expect others to act according to a common standard, which makes it irrational to subject oneself to the standard. On the other hand, in societies in which rules are customarily obeyed, it is reasonable to submit to these.

---

[31] B. Kliksberg y L. Tomassini (Comps.), *Capital Social y Cultura*, Buenos Aires, F.C.E. / BID, 2000.

At this point I should like to remind readers that norms form the skeleton of a society, that in spite of the fact that the term "rule" has unpleasant connotations for large sectors of the population, what is true is that rules are only the reciprocal expectations of widespread action. Without such expectations, there is no society.[32]

One important rule in this sphere is that self-interest must be waived, acting in the group's interest. A rule like this, reinforced by social support, status, honour and other rewards, is the social capital constructed by young nations, strengthening families and facilitating the development of social movements, but tending to be seen only when these are in their infancy, and later fading.

In some cases rules are internalised; in others, supported by external rewards for disinterested actions and by acts of disapproval for the selfish. In both cases these are important to overcome problems involving public goods, precisely because public goods are ones which can be enjoyed by a large number of persons, though not all contribute to producing them.

Indeed, investments in financial and human capital benefit those who make them, but the type of social structures which make social standards and the penalties which reinforce them possible benefit all those who form part of the structure. Since the benefits affect persons other than the agent (unlike the case with private capital), these persons are often not interested in creating them, if our method for explaining human action is methodological individualism. From this standpoint, three replies have been given to the question about the formation of social capital: 1) Most forms of social capital are created and destroyed as by-products of other activities. This is the reply given by Coleman, amongst others. 2) The institutions create structures which save transaction costs, because an external agent (it may be the State) coerces by means of penalties. 3) The game theory, in its different versions, displays the advantages of cooperating and the disadvantages of not doing so.[33]

Nevertheless, a fourth reply is possible, which is that sometimes there could be a moment of intentional altruism in the production of public goods, an investment meant to create wealth in benefit of others, including free ridery.

At this point I should like to point out how Amartya Sen goes as far as asserting that those who run a company which operates ethically are also producing a public good, although the company is private, because getting just relations under way, generating trust and fostering credibility in mutual relations is tantamount to investing in a social capital which benefits society as a whole, and not only the company which creates this.

---

[32] J. Habermas, *Faktizität und Geltung*, 138.

[33] F. Herreros and A. de Francisco, "Introducción: el capital social como programa de investigación", in issue 94/95 (2001) of *Zona abierta* (pp. 1-45), on social capital, monographically.

As I see it, reminding companies that they should assume corporate responsibility for their actions includes the responsibility for generating social capital.

Nevertheless, as we have already mentioned, social capital has its light and dark sides. Effective norms, which may constitute a form of social capital which facilitates certain action, may prevent other action, create social inertia, reluctant to adopt any form of innovation, although this ultimately would end up benefiting the population as a whole, and can also lead to consecrating certain types of conduct as "normal" and others as "deviant".

This is why it is advisable to carefully analyse social structures which on one hand facilitate social capital and may, on the other, end up choking people's autonomy and creativity.

For example, Glucksman distinguishes between *simplex* and *multiplex* relations, and understands that the latter generate greater social capital, because people are bonded in more than one context in them, as occurs at a school, where pupils' parents are linked by relationships of neighbourhood, work, friendship and religion. In such cases abandonment and dropout rates are lower. But one could also think that these contexts do not always favour freedom and innovation.

Coleman mentions the closure of social networks, on which effective norms depend, as one of the types of social structure which particularly facilitate social capital. Closure is the action which imposes external effects on others, and is a necessary but not sufficient condition.

5.   From social capital to social wealth

Social capital may in theory be a resource for people, but may also be such for "corporate actors", also existing in the relations between organisations, which can also be actors. As far as *people* are concerned, they can and do in fact use certain aspects of social structure as resources for realising their interests. Assuming the standpoint of methodological individualism it is possible to examine which social relations can be capital resources for individuals, but it is none the less true that methodological individualism does not go far enough on occasions.

As far as institutions are concerned, the central premise of the theory of social capital can be summed up in the affirmation that social connections and civic commitment have an influence on both our public life and private projects; that there is a relationship between economic Modernity, institutional performance and civil community.

In a society with social capital it is easier to live, amongst other reasons, because the dilemmas of collective action are easier to settle, and because incentives and opportunism are reduced. The creation of virtuous circles, as dealt with in Chapter 2 of this book, makes it reasonable to act according to common standards and to dissuade free ridery from breaking the rules.

On the other hand, networks of civic commitment embody the cooperation that was a success in the past and which can act as a cultural pattern for future cooperation work, there being a crystallisation of the measures that have given the best results and which make it advisable to extend cooperation networks.

However, the fundamental reason why social capital allows a solution to the dilemmas of collective action, such as Arrow's famous Impossibility Theorem, is that the dense networks of interaction probably extend the sense of the self, developing the *"I"* into *"us"* or, in the language of theorists of collective action, refining the "taste" for collective benefits. This is, in my view, the reason why both republicans and communitarians are interested in fostering social capital: because the only way to settle dilemmas of collective action is not to balance collective interests in the liberal fashion, but to transform the "I" into "us". Do any forms of social relations allow this transformation?

According to R.D. Putnam, the very act of association is what facilitates social cooperation advancing towards democracy, more than the objectives of associations. Associative density is already a factor for democracy to work. Nevertheless Putnam is severely criticised on this point, and I would also disagree: it is not true that all kinds of associations create social capital, at least the type of social capital located on the post-conventional level in the development of the social moral conscience, which is the only sort that can favour the working of politics practiced by autonomous and supportive citizens and of an economy aware of its debt with all human beings.

This is why one ought to acknowledge that not all associations are capable of creating social capital in the aforementioned sense, but only those with at least the following features:[34]

1) If we distinguish between horizontal and vertical associations, as Putnam does in *Making Democracy Work*, horizontal associations are the ones that favour a politics of autonomous and supportive beings. Horizontal associations are the kind that "unite agents with equivalent status and power", while vertical ones "combine unequal agents in symmetrical relations of hierarchy and dependency". The latter clearly have a very limited capacity of generating relations of reciprocity, mutuality and cooperation. Since reaching acceptable decisions for all is what helps to overcome collective problems, resorting to vertical organisations is not something that favours cooperation. One should also distinguish between associations by the aims of the group and depending on their capacity to promote cooperation. In this respect three types of relations can be distinguished:

---

[34] C. Boix, "El concepto de capital social y sus implicaciones económicas, in R.D. Putnam, *Per a fer que la democràcia funcioni*, Barcelona, Proa, 2000, pp. 13-49.

2) It is clear that groups which foster intolerance and inequality among their members have a negative impact on social capital.
3) The objective of cooperation may be harmful or beneficial for the community. Mafias or the Ku Klux Klan are clearly harmful, while the Sisters of the Poor are beneficial. The fact of social capital existing does not mean that this is used for the good of the community.
4) Associations are also distinguished from one another according to whether the social capital which is created in the group is useful or not in the interactions which take place inside this. Putnam distinguishes between "social capital which lays bridges" and "the sort that does not lay bridges". A society consisting of powerful associations which collide with each other is destructive.
5) And lastly, it seems that the associations which produce public wealth generate greater social capital than the ones which produce private wealth. It seems that the former should create more social capital, while the latter foster opportunist conduct.

Nevertheless, we should in my opinion remember that the associations which produce public goods are not identified simply with the ones that manage public resources, and that the associations which produce private goods cannot simply be identified with the ones that manage private resources. An association of the first kind may mainly seek its members' private interests, and one of the second type can generate honest conduct, which generate credibility and trust and thus produce a public good.

From all this it follows that social capital is generated by the type of associations which embody the values of a *civic ethics*, which we shall deal with in part five of this book. That is, associations which foster their members' autonomy, equality and solidarity. These are thus horizontal, fostering mutual respect among their members, proving to be beneficial for society as a whole, generating a solidarity which is not enclosed within the limits of that association, but influencing the rest of society, constituting a public good because they create habits of trust and solidarity.

Indeed, social capital may be taken as a resource, just like physical and human resources. In this respect, I would again remind you of the Kantian metaphor of the people of devils, which would prefer cooperation to conflict, on condition that they were intelligent. The intangible hand of shared virtues and values saves coordination costs and for this reason would have to be of interest to intelligent devils.

Indeed, as far as the *economy* is concerned, this activity that positivists of all ages have described as "neutral", as alien to values, as a mere mechanism subjected to almost natural laws, proves actually to be quite the opposite to the positivists' claims, and it turns out that without physical resources the economy does not work, but neither does it work without human resources, without social resources, without shared values, without habits generating the trust required to sign a contract with certain guarantees of compliance, without some dose of honesty and loyalty, without that dense fabric of human associations which actually forms the most plentiful wealth of nations and peoples. Without social capital there are not even businesses in this globalised universe, in which the protective network of values and associations provides the essential ground for transactions and contracts to work properly.

But the same thing happens with the strength of *democratic politics*, which seems to depend on activities of political parties and governments, when what is actually true is that it depends to a large extent on *civil society*, on its values and its *associative capacity*, on social capital: on society, in short.

Indeed, the fruitfulness of social capital for both generating a genuine democracy, in which the people are the central actors, and for laying the foundations of an efficient and just economy, of an economy in the full sense of the world, is one of the central subjects for study in social sciences. But the reality of the associations to which we have referred is not maintained only by self-interest, is not only maintained by the inertia of finding itself already tangled in a virtuous circle. It is not only a *resource*, but an *asset*, not only a strategy, but an *êthos*, a character, a form of *wealth*.

Human rationality is not only strategic, not only prudential even, this being the reason for the limitations of methodological individualism and economic imperialism. The reality of the associations referred to above is maintained by wealth, by a set of shared values, one of which is the value of associating with another at one's own choice.

In this respect, it would not be inappropriate, as we head into the new century, to consider the advisability of "inverting Tocqueville", at least partly, recognising that in certain crucial aspects it is not North America which has a more powerful social capital, but precisely Europe, and that it is important not to let this dilapidate, lest it be impossible to set it up again later on.

There are doubtlessly regions with a great *associative capacity* in Europe, and it is urgent to stimulate this "associative art", by extending it to more individualistic regions and making this material in institutions. But all of this must be done from the *values* (the other side of social capital) which part of Europe has shared throughout its history and which constitute its greatest "competitive advantage" over other political and economic centres.

Europe's *competitive advantage* cannot consist in copying (like the old Spanish maxim "Let the others invent things!"), but in fulfilling its own dream: the "European dream" of a just and efficient society, where efficiency has justice as its aim, and where efficiency is achieved precisely from justice. An unjust society is ultimately not even efficient, since justice, valuable in itself, is also a "tool" to optimise physical and human resources, because it gives greater cohesion to a society than its opposite.

The European dream includes foundations of security for citizens and for immigrants, which cannot be maintained without radical reforms, but which are also unrenounceable. Milestones on the way to fulfilment of this dream would be stable but flexible employment, health care provided by a public network from an efficient and fair public management system, quality education which universally distributes good "know-how", being able to trust in finding protective cover when one leaves paid work behind and in old age, the security of being given properly treated as any human being deserves, simply through being human, when hunger and misery force one to abandon one's own land. The "free world", or at least the one that preaches freedom, ought to be reminded that the most basic of freedoms is the "freedom from need". Only countries which practice this inside and outside their frontiers really have a social capital able to create internal cohesion and external cooperation, able to lay the foundations for practising freedom. When they eventually talk of this and propose it they would be at last designing a round circle.

IV. Political community
and ethical community

7. POLITICAL COMMUNITY AND ETHICAL COMMUNITY

1. Abstract universality, concrete communities

The history of philosophy, as Kant so rightly pointed out in the first Critique, is in some way the history of disputes between different philosophical positions.[1] In recent times, as far as the sphere of practical philosophy is concerned, at least three overall themes have acted as the apple of discord; the design of a notion of *justice*, appropriate for societies with liberal democracy; polemics between universalists and communitarians about the importance of the concrete *communities* in the configuration of the person; and lastly, the discussion about the concept of *citizenship*, which can also generate a feeling of belonging in the members of societies with liberal democracy, legitimated by principles of justice. The frequent controversies on multiculturalism are obviously closely related with these three great subjects, but very particularly in connection with the idea of citizenship; a multicultural — or better still, intercultural — citizenship seems to have become essential.[2]

As regards the discussion between communitarianism and universalism, we should remember how the Anglo-Saxon controversy tends to centre more on the "communitarism-individualism" discussion, as communitarians accuse liberals of taking the individual as an ontological and ethical nucleus of society, when it is actually true that the individual becomes a person inside concrete communities. In fact, A. MacIntyre's criticisms are aimed at emotivist individualism, in which liberalism comes out; an individualism which puts rules before virtues. Sandel, on the other hand, criticises that "self without attributes" which from the original position chooses principles of justice, when what really matter are the "concrete selves", the persons born and growing up in particular communities.

The German world approaches, and continues to approach, the dispute of communitarianism around two flags: that of Kant and that of Hegel.[3] Kant

---

[1] The origin of this chapter is in "La paz en Kant: Ética y Política" (in V. Martínez (ed.), *Kant: La paz perpetua, doscientos años después*, Valencia, Nau, 1997, pp. 69-82) and in "El comunitarismo universalista de la filosofía kantiana", (in J. Carvajal (coord.), *Moral, derecho y política en Immanuel Kant*, Cuenca, Universidad de Castilla-La Mancha, 1999, pp. 241-252).

[2] I dealt with outlining a theory of citizenship and developing its different aspects in detail in *Ciudadanos del mundo*.

[3] W. Kuhlmann (Hg.), *Moralität und Sittlichkeit*, Frankfurt, Suhrkamp, 1986; A. Cortina, *Ética sin moral*, chap. 4.

represents the universalism of the "moral standpoint", the abstraction proper to "Moralität"; while Hegel, in the tracks of Aristotle, defends the supremacy of the *êthos* of peoples, the concrete reality of "Sittlichkeit".[4]

Hegel would not give any credit to the contractualists who think that individuals seal an agreement of convenience to form the State, because the State is prior to individuals, the *polis* being the nutritious earth in which concrete people are formed. In our times, the differences between universalists and communitarians are approached under the respective auspices of Kant and Hegel. Are both of them right? Is it impossible to find a mediating element?

The reply to this question is affirmative, as I see it, and it is precisely Kantian philosophy which most clearly shows the possibility of linking moral universalism with the vital role played by communities in moralising people.[5] Kant's philosophy does not exude abstract universalism, demeaning the importance of communities for moralising specific people, quite the opposite.

This is the reason why a very similar position is defended today by some of the most relevant "Kantian" ethics, as is the case of discourse ethics, which also lays a bridge between abstract universalism and specific communities. First of all, because the outset of philosophical reflection — in the case of discourse ethics — is not the individual, but rather *intersubjectivity, reciprocal recognition* of two beings endowed with communicative competence, who recognise each others' capacity to raise claims to validity and to offer a reasoned reply, in the event of any of these being put in doubt. If this were not enough, as soon as those who communicate use a linguistic rule, they recognise through this their belonging to a *community* of talkers, who also make use of such a rule. Taking a third step, the only way of elucidating if a norm of action is valid and if a proposition is true consists in resorting to a discourse which ultimately counterfactually presupposes an *ideal community of argumentation* so, to agree in this with Apel, the ideal communication community constitutes a counterfactual anticipation of reason.

And the point is indeed that it proves just as impossible to rationally opt for a strictly conventional communitarianism on Kohlberg's scale, deprived of any claim to universality, as it is irrational to opt for a universalism alien to concrete communities. This has brought about the tendency for universalists and communitarians to see their standpoints converge over time, until reaching this hybridism which is ultimately rationally inevitable.[6] But in this

---

    [4] G.W.F. Hegel, *Grundlinien der Philosophie des Rechts*, §33.

    [5] For similar mediation from the Hegelian position, see V. Hösle, *Hegels System. Der Idealismus der Subjektivität und das Problem der Intersubjektivität*, Hamburg, Meiner, 1987; R.B. Pippin, "What is the Question for which Hegel's Theory of Recognition is the Answer?", in *European Journal of Philosophy*, 8/2 (2000), pp. 155-172.

    [6] A. Cortina, *Ética aplicada y democracia radical*, pp. 79 ff.

case such hybridism was in some way already present in the practical philosophy of Kant, undoubtedly one of the most eminent representatives of moral universalism.

2.   The ideal of the kingdom of ends

If we look at the Kantian moral works from the critical period, we will find that the first two formulations of the categorical imperative- those of Universality and of the End in itself — tackle universality from the moral standpoint, and also deal with its intersubjective nature, but not its communitarian dimension. The test of these first two formulations of the imperative induces the moral subject to attempt to intersubjectivise his maxima, to attempt to find out if, when doing this, it proves contradictory or not, either with thought or volition. Intersubjectivity and not individualism is thus the key to Kantian philosophy, in which Hegel would abound, since a maxima will not display any value as a moral law if it does not display its rational character, the reason being precisely the faculty of the intersubjective. And in this respect, it is astounding to see how Apel and Habermas insist on accusing Kant of practising a curious subjectivism, when the key to Kantian philosophy is intersubjectivity.[7]

Nevertheless, going back to the first two formulations of the imperative, what cannot be said about these is that they should take into account the communitarian nature of the moral subject. It would in any event be the formulation of the Kingdom of Ends which could take on a communitarian dimension, as this formulation forces us to organise coexistence in such a way that it is possible to deal with each rational being as an end in himself, which requires taking into account, even though formally, the subjective ends which each individual sets himself. Indeed, to remember Kant's words about the Kingdom of Ends:

> "By a *kingdom* I understand the union of different rational beings in a system by common laws. Now since it is by laws that ends are determined as regards their universal validity, hence, if we abstract from the personal differences of rational beings and likewise from all the content of their private ends, we shall be able to conceive all ends combined in a systematic whole (including both rational beings as ends in themselves, and also the special ends which each may propose to himself), that is to say, we can conceive a kingdom of ends, which on the preceding principles is possible".[8]

---

[7] J. Habermas has changed his mind in *Die Zukunft der menschlichen Natur. Auf dem Weg zu einer liberalen Eugenik?* Frankfurt, Suhrkamp, 2001.

[8] I. Kant, *Grundlegung zur Metaphysik der Sitten*, Kants Werke, IV, Part II.

To be anything more than just a word devoid of content, respecting rational beings as ends in themselves requires us to take the fact that they are going to set themselves subjective ends seriously and even without specifying what these are materially, establishing a systematic union between them "by common objective laws" as is stated in the paragraph after the one quoted. That is, by laws which allow those who are ends in themselves to attain their subjective ends, without preventing others from attaining them too, but instead fostering the possibility for both to do this.[9] What is the gnoseological statute of this kingdom of ends? Is this a concept, an idea or an ideal?

The answer of the *Fundamental Principles of the Metaphysics of Morals* is clear: the notion of a pure intelligible world, like an ensemble of all the intelligences, is an idea of reason. A universal kingdom of ends in themselves, "to which we can all belong as members when we behave carefully according to maxima of freedom", is an ideal; that is — following the indications of the *Critique of Pure Reason*, the idea embodied in some kind of entity. In the case of the first Critique, the idea of *omnitudo realitatis*, the idea of a "sum-total of reality", is embodied in the ideal of pure reason, that is of God. In the case of practical reason, the idea of an intelligible world is embodied in the ideal of a rational community: in the ideal of a kingdom of ends in themselves.[10]

Indeed, the ideal of the kingdom of ends has been a principle inspiring political utopias, of which neo-Kantian socialism is a very clear example, seeing as it did the aim of history in this.[11] Nevertheless, attaining a similar ideal demands, from a Kantian standpoint, reality and promotion of a very specific type of community: the *ethical community*, as this is designed above all in *Religion within the limits of mere reason*.

3. **Radical evil**

It is in point of fact in this work that Kant tackles the most serious problem facing ethics: in human beings there is an innate propensity to give priority to the maxima of selfishness over moral law, a propensity which constitutes what

---

[9] This is one of the reasons why it seems difficult to me (with Hegel) to distinguish two stages in Kantian ethics (A. Heller, *Crítica de la Ilustración*, Barcelona, Península, 1984, chap. II). I understand on the other hand that between the *Grundlegund zur Metaphysik der Sitten* and the second Critique, on one hand, and *Die Metaphysik der Sitten*, on the other, there is only one basic difference: *Die Metaphysik der Sitten* attempts to put forward the System of Morals, and not only to outline the critique. But as regards ethical conception, the difference is more of accent than of stage.

[10] I. Kant, *Grundlegung zur Metaphysik der Sitten*, Kants Werke, IV, Chap. 3.

[11] K. Vorländer, "Kant und Marx", Tübingen, Paul Siebeck, J.C.B. Mohr, 1911 y 1926 (in Socialismo y ética, Madrid, Pluma/Debate, 1980, pp. 157-198).

Kant calls "radical evil". The idea of radical evil is present in all Kant's practical work, and stems from a tradition originating in Saint Augustine, taken up again by Luther: man is made of crooked wood and nothing straight can be fashioned from this.[12] How can he possibly overcome his innate predisposition towards evil and opt for the moral law which is definitively his own law?

Conversion (*Umwandlung*) of the heart is the only way. Transformation of the intention is the only thing that can allow human beings to be free.[13] And the greatness and misery of morality consists of the fact that this transformation can never come from outside, because neither changes in political structures, nor all humanity's efforts can make a person's heart change, if that person does not wish it to.

Nevertheless, Kant would add, what is indeed impossible for an individual without help from outside is to keep the willingness to act correctly, for it is actually relations with other human beings which lead each one to become corrupt. As soon as we embark on relations, envy, the desire for dominance, covetousness, and hostile inclinations all begin to emerge in us. For this reason, individual ethics prove to be insufficient for attaining one's own perfection, which is the first of the duties of virtue,[14] and the support of a "community ethics" is thus required; the person's faithfulness to virtue requires fostering a type of union between men whose raison d'être consists in maintaining morality in every one of these. This is why Kant expressly asserts:

> "As far as we can see, therefore, the sovereignty of the good principle is attainable, so far as men can work toward it, only through the establishment and spread of a society in accordance with, and for the sake of, the laws of virtue, a society whose task and duty it is rationally to impress these laws in all their scope upon the entire human race".".[15]

This "society according to and for the sake of laws of virtue" forms an "ethical society or community", which is not identified with political community, though there are analogies between them. What makes them similar and what makes them different?

4. Political civil state — ethical civil state

The *ethical community* constitutes what Kant himself calls an "*ethical civil state*", an expression which is not common in the world of moral philosophy.

---

[12] A. Nygren, *Eros et Agape*, París, 1944, pp. 286 and 287.
[13] I. Kant, *Die Religion innerhalb der Grenzen der blossen Vernunft*, (= *Religion*), VI, pp. 47-48.
[14] I. Kant, *Die Metaphysik der Sitten*, VI, pp. 391 and ff.
[15] I. Kant, *Religion*, p. 94.

This means that those who are governed by its laws have moved on from a *"ethical state of nature"* to an *"ethical civil state"* in the same way as a political civil State, a Constitutional State, stems from the wish to depart from a state of legal nature. What is the reason that has led citizens in each of these forms of civil state to wanting to abandon the state of nature?

In the case of the state of legal nature, what moves potential citizens to seal the social covenant is the desire to have what each one considers as being their own legally guaranteed. Kant in this case develops the tradition of Hobbes and Pufendorf, according to whom the state of nature is a state of potential war, and understands that in this state individuals can claim their property, but only provisionally, which is why it is of interest to them to go into a civil state, in which each individual can defend their property legally. While there is no civil state people cannot defend what they have acquired depending on "the endorsement of a public law, because this is not determined by a public (distributive) justice nor assured by any power which exercises this right".[16] The contract to be governed by common and public laws is what marks the move on from the political state of nature to the political civil state.

What is the distinctive factor of an ethical civil state as opposed to a ethical state of nature?

> "The ethical state of nature — Kant would say expressly- is an *open* conflict between the principles of virtue and a state of inner amorality, which the natural man ought to bestir himself to leave as soon as possible".[17]

In this state of nature it is moral evil which attacks individuals, who not only fail to help each other to overcome it, but increase the common discouragement. It is thus a moral duty to attempt to leave this ethical state of nature and form a community which is governed by *public laws*, as the move from nature to civility is marked by the sign of publicity.

> "A union of men under merely moral laws, patterned on the above idea, may be called an *ethical*, and so far as these laws are public, an *ethico-civil* (in contrast to a *juridico-civil*) *society* or an *ethical commonwealth*. It can exist in the midst of a political commonwealth [...] It has, however, a special and unique principle of union (virtue), and hence a form and constitution, which fundamentally distinguish it from the political commonwealth"[18]

The *publicity* of laws is thus the distinctive trait of any civil state, both the political and the ethical kind. But there are considerable differences between both types of state, which we could sum up in four categories: the type of

---

[16] I. Kant, *Die Metaphysik der Sitten*, VI, p. 312.
[17] I. Kant, *Religion*, VI, p. 97.
[18] *Ibid.*, 94.

motive which leads to found each of these, the nature of *coercion* which gives compulsoriness of the laws, the type of *assent* which can be received from the members of the community and the *extension* of the validity of laws.

As far as the extension of the validity of ethical laws is concerned, this should obviously be universal. While a political community has the priority obligation of defending its members and thus intends its norms to be valid for citizens — which Habermas would call "Rechtsgenossen"—, moral laws are characterised precisely by claiming to be of universal value: through referring to a republic of humanity as a whole.[19]

As regards the *motive*, those who become part of a political civil state aspire to legally defend property and to free themselves from having to do this by war, property also referring to life itself. While in the state of nature a member of society cannot defend their property other than provisionally, in the political civil state they can defend this legally.[20] The motive of those who become part of an ethical civil state is to help themselves to overcome moral evil, which consists in the propensity to opt for selfishness and not for the law of freedom.[21]

However, the deepest difference between the ethical civil community and the political one refers to the type of *coercion* and *assent* which goes with the law. Because in the case of the laws of virtue, however much these may be public, both the acceptance of the validity of the law and the coercion which obliges us to obey this have to be internal. If a moral subject is not persuaded that a maxima of their action can become a moral law, no force outside their conscience can impose this on them morally. If a moral subject does not undergo remorse — internal punishment — for having broken a moral rule, there is no external penalty which can punish them morally. The members of an ethical community, however much they might wish to, cannot morally coerce the other members for them to act according to laws of virtue, because moral coercion is internal. But, quite the opposite, the members of the political community can indeed legally coerce other citizens for them to obey "juridical laws" and respect the legal freedom of the whole political body.

This is why the laws of virtue set out to promote interior morality, the goodness of will, while juridical laws are intended to guarantee the practice of outside liberty,[22] for which purpose it is essential to ensure lasting peace. Are the

---

[19] J. Habermas, *Faktizität und Geltung*, p. 139.

[20] I. Kant, *Die Metaphysik der Sitten*, VI, p. 312.

[21] The Kantian ethic is more "*eleuteronomic*" than "deontological", as is shown by J. Conill in *El enigma del animal fantástico*, Madrid, Tecnos, 1991, and in "Eleuteronomía y antroponomía en la filosofía práctica de Kant", in J. Carvajal (coord.), *Moral, derecho y política en Kant*, pp. 265-284.

[22] I. Kant, *Die Metaphysik der Sitten*, VI, p. 214.

ethical community and the political community thus parallel, in such a way that each of these has its target (overcoming moral evil, in one case, and establishing peace in the other)?

5. Ethical community and political community

"A *juridico-civil (political) state* is the relation of men to each other in which they all alike stand socially under *public juridical laws* (which are, as a class, laws of coercion). An *ethico-civil state* is that in which they are united under non-coercive laws, i.e., *laws of virtue* alone."[23]

Indeed, the relations between ethical and political community should be relations of mutual respect. The political community can never force its citizens to enter an ethical community, because in the latter freedom should prevail against any coercion. However much the governor may want virtue to dominate in the spirits of his citizens (because wherever coercion has no success, virtue can help to comply with the laws) what is indeed true is that the political community can never impose its laws on the ethical community.

On the other hand, the ethical community, governed by public laws of virtue, is a part of different political communities. And here we find once more the problem posed by Saint Augustine and taken up later by Martin Luther: the problem of the two kingdoms, of the two worlds. The political world cannot impose its laws on the world of inner freedom, but neither can public laws of the ethical world break political laws. The Lutheran notion of the autonomy of the political sphere remains in Kantian philosophy, neutralising — whether for good or for bad — the reiterated accusation that the Kantian may practice the "terror of virtue".[24]

Quite the opposite, as Vlachos quite rightly points out, Kantian philosophy is revolutionary when we restrict ourselves to the strictly ethical works, but becomes conservative in juridical and political works. In these, following the Lutheran tradition, he respects the autonomy of the political order against the Church (Luther)[25] or against the Church and the moral world (Kant). One cannot expect the Kantian to resist political power nor to question the death penalty.[26] The revolution of the heart and the freedom of the pen are the only terrors which virtue allows itself against political order.

The public laws of the ethical community thus have to respect the political laws, something difficult to do on many occasions, but also have to extend to

---

[23] I. Kant, *Religion*, p. 95.
[24] W. Kuhlmann, *Moralität und Sittlichkeit*, 10.
[25] S. Wolin, *Politics and vision*, Boston, Little, Brown and Company, 1960, chap. 5.
[26] I. Kant, *Die Metaphysik der Sitten*, VI, pp. 318 and ff.

all humanity, attempting to promote morality in actions. However, since morality is internal, the ethical community can submit to public laws, but not human ones; it will submit to the laws of God's people, laws which nevertheless have to be discovered by each human subject as moral laws in their heart. The dimension of publicity of laws thus has an educational role, but on condition that the subject recognises them as being good.

However, the particular constitution of moral laws repeatedly leads to paradoxical situations, as on one hand it is each human subject who has to recognise the obligatory nature of the law, and on the other hand, it proves extremely difficult to personally recognise this obligatory nature in deeply discouraged societies, in which moral laws are widely disdained. Someone who has to assume the task of verifying if a maxima can or not become a moral law, will not even bother to attempt this if he has not learned to positively value that kind of law throughout the socialisation process, if the society in which he lives is not publicly interested in this.

The feeling of respect is, according to Kant, intellectual, but does not require any less cultivation for this reason. It constitutes, as Kant himself asserts, one of the aesthetic conditions of morality, because without this feeling the flesh and blood person is unable to perceive the greatness of his freedom, the greatness of his own law, and thus unable to take any interest in this.[27] However, as is obvious, it proves practically impossible to cultivate this feeling of respect in a "demoralised" society, to put this in Ortega's terms; in a society in which it is publicly accepted that selfish interest is the sole really rational motive of conducts.

Hence the publicity of moral laws has the educational power which accompanies what is socially positively valued as desirable, the educational quality of what is considered a good that has to be attained in a society. This cannot be achieved if it is not through this community, which has departed from the state of moral nature, and expresses its adhesion to a civic morality, a morality of citizens.

Because although it is true that each person and each time should have its learning, it proves difficult to go ahead with this when *ideas do not coincide with beliefs*. Ortega quite rightly says that we *have* ideas and we *are* beliefs.[28] And it proves almost impossible to educate in the aforementioned approaches when there is an abyss between the ideas of a society and the beliefs by which one acts.

This is why, to *make beliefs match ideas*, though he never said this in so many words, Kant proposed in the late 18th century creating an "ethical civil state", an "ethical civil society". Incorporating moral universality entails the

---

[27] I. Kant, *Die Metaphysik der Sitten*, VI, pp. 399-403.

[28] J. Ortega y Gasset, *Ideas y Creencias*, in *Obras completas*, V, Madrid, Revista de Occidente, 1940, 377-409.

need for *creating specific ethical communities* which, precisely through being ethical, can never renounce the standpoint of universality. No form of communitarianism and no republicanism that does not wish to be criticised as merely reactionary would dare to deny this today.

This is the reason why, in my opinion, one should educate not only in pure universalism nor in prudish communitarianism, but in deeply-rooted cosmopolitanism.

8. EDUCATING IN DEEP-ROOTED COSMOPOLITANISM

1. Education in the moral values of a pluralist society

The origins of religious and moral pluralism in the western world date back to the 16th and 17th centuries, when the bloody outcome of the religious wars, or rather, of the psychological, economic and political wars dressed up in religious garb, gradually revealed the absurdity of intolerance in questions of convictions.[29] It did not seem very much in keeping with the spirit of Christianity to torture or kill dissidents merely through dissenting, when the deepest message of the Gospel was precisely love. Christian thinkers such as John Locke, or deists such as Voltaire, amongst others, engendered the publications on tolerance which might originally still have been fairly intolerant, but which gave rise in time to the acceptance of pluralism. Tolerating the plurality of ultimate conceptions, the diversity of world views, gradually became a natural situation for a human society.

It is true that the advancing tide of history has its ebbs and flows, just as it is that different western societies accepted moral pluralism as a natural fact at diverse times. In fact in Spain the "normalisation" of moral pluralism did not start seriously until 1978, when the Constitution officially acknowledged what was already a social fact, that in Spain people practised more than one religion, or none at all, and that they lived their lives under diverse moralities.

This new situation obviously gave rise to some new problems which I have been tackling for some time now,[30] but in this chapter I should like to refer only to one of them, which is that of moral education. It is readily understandable that in a "morally monist" society, that is one with a single moral code, not too many difficulties are involved in deciding what morality to educate

---

[29] This chapter comes from A. Cortina, "¿Educación para el patriotismo o para el cosmopolitismo?", in A. Cortina (coord.), *La educación y los valores*, Madrid, Fundación Argentaria/ Biblioteca Nueva, 2000, pp. 61-80.

[30] A. Cortina, *Ética mínima* (1986); *Ética aplicada y democracia radical* (1993); *La ética de la sociedad civil* (1994); *El quehacer ético. Una guía para la educación moral*, Madrid, Santillana, 1995; *Ciudadanos como protagonistas* 1999.

children and young people in, because the real or officially accepted code is the one that supplies patterns for moral education. However, in pluralist societies the first problem found in this field consists in explaining which values one must educate in as a society, which have to be conveyed in public education and in centres with a specific ideology, since the question "what values do we want to convey in education?" forces a society to become aware of which values are the ones that it really appreciates.

A thread had to be found to gradually unravel the matter, and the first one which education specialists came up with was the "*value clarification*" method. After years of authoritarianism, society shunned any kind of indoctrination, any attempt to force children and young people to accept a vital structure beyond which it was impossible for them to think, which is why the clarification of values seemed the most respectful procedure to accompany the child in the Socratic process of making him or herself. The method consisted in helping children to fully understand the values that they had learned at their homes or with their friends and which they had taken in with no further discernment, trusting that understanding their real meaning and consequences would lead the child to reject what is to be rejected and accept what is desirable.[31]

Nevertheless, the clarification of values proved to be more of a useful technique than a real educational method because, taken as a method, this inevitably produced a sensation of relativism and subjectivism, totally alien to what is really the experience of morality. Slaughter, hunger, torture, disloyalty and corruption do not make people react by shrugging their shoulders indifferently, but with indignation or with shame, both indicating that relativism and subjectivism are inhuman, and that moral questions are not "highly subjective", but "highly intersubjective".

Proceduralism stepped in to replace the clarification of values, claiming the guarantee of its excellent philosophical pedigree, that of stemming from the ethical theories of Kantian formalism, amongst others, the ethics of discourse and Rawls' theory of justice. As opposed to *substantialism*, unsustainable in a pluralist society because it attempts to convey an idea of good life *with content*, when different proposals of a happy life cohabit in a pluralist society, *proceduralism* understands that morality already impregnates everyday life in the form of behavioural norms, which allow us to organise our reciprocal expectations. What really matters is discovering the procedures required to discern which of the norms in force are also valid. When a norm is questioned, it is important to find out what the proper procedure is to determine if this is *just*

---

[31] J. Escámez, "Teorías contemporáneas sobre educación moral", in J. Escámez, E. Pérez, *Un mundo de valores*, chapter 4; J.M. Puig Rovira, *La construcción de la personalidad moral*, Barcelona, Paidós, 1996, chapter 1.

or not. Matters of justice constitute the key to shared life, which is why children and young people should be educated in the readiness to go by rational procedures to discover what norms are just and what unfair.

Nevertheless, proceduralism came in for a lot of criticism, not only from outside, but also from within its own proposal.[32] No matter how respectful procedures may seem to be with the pluralism of conceptions of good life, no matter how disassociated from values (such an elusive world) they may claim to be, the truth is that people are not moved by procedures, however rational these may seem: nobody makes a revolution through a procedure. People get into action through the desire to embody *values* or obtain *goods*, and procedures are only useful for enabling us to discover where justice lies, *justice being a value*, thus endowed with the dynamic power to stimulate conduct.

It was thus important to bring the world of values back up, but not by juxtaposing these, like an aggregate, but along a guiding thread which would enable finding out which should be universally conveyed. The notion of citizenship then arose again, a notion at least as ancient as political life in classical Greece, not to speak of the East, which came this time to give help in the sphere of moral education. Schooling should teach in the values of citizenship, as being a good citizen is something that can be required of anyone who lives in a political community. The question now becomes one of knowing which values the genuine citizen should accept.

2. The values of citizenship

The problem is nevertheless that as soon as an end is found to start unravelling the moral thread in which education should be given, difficulties start to come up. The first of these consists in this case in choosing the model of citizenship in which to educate, because since the *polítes* of Pericles' Athens and the *civis* of classical Rome countless models of citizenship have succeeded one another and mingled in the history of the west.[33] The second difficulty involves considering the different dimensions of citizenship from the legal and political sides to the social, multicultural and differentiated aspects, a question which I already looked into elsewhere.[34]

---

[32] K.O. Apel, A. Cortina, J. De Zan and D. Michelini (eds.), *Ética comunicativa y Democracia*, Barcelona, Crítica, 1991.

[33] D. Heather, *Citizenship*, London/New York, Longman, 1990; J.G.A. Pocock, "The Ideal of Citizenship Since Classical Times", in R. Beiner (ed.), *Theorizing Citizenship*, State of New York Press, 1995, 29-52.

[34] A. Cortina, *Ciudadanos del mundo*, Madrid, Alianza, 1997.

But thirdly, to complete the range of issues open when the concept of citizenship is brought up again, a question which the North American world formulates in the following terms emerges: when we educate in citizenship, should we educate for patriotism or for cosmopolitanism? Such a question seems in theory to be perfectly appropriate for the United States and Latin-American world, but not so much for Europe, in which the blunt approach of patriotic obligations seems rather obsolete. In fact, when A. MacIntyre published a work entitled "Is Patriotism a Virtue?",[35] its very title looked strange in Europe: how can one seriously ask if patriotism is a virtue and the lack of patriotism a vice? What does this "patriotism" mean?

Nevertheless, calm reflection on the concept of citizenship, in any of its versions, discovers that the question is not obsolete even in Europe, nor a trivial matter, but one that involves a real problem for liberal democratic societies as a whole in whatever terms it may be presented, because the notion of citizenship contains in theory the germ of the tendency to create closed communities.

Indeed a "citizen" is someone who belongs as a full member to a particular political community, with which he or she has undertaken a commitment to special obligations of loyalty.[36] The notion of "belonging" not only involves a feeling of being rooted in a particular political community, but also the awareness of having responsibilities, obligations of loyalty in respect of that community. The idea of citizenship then, is developed from the "internal/external", "identity/difference", "inclusion/exclusion" contrasts, from the recognition that the members of the community have identifying traits which distinguish them from those who are not members of it. In the very act of knowing that they are identical with each other they know themselves to be different from those who are beyond the community's limits. *The identifying fact is at the same time the differentiating fact.*

If this is the way things are, what should we take as a starting point for education in citizenship values: the ones proper to local citizenship, "those of patriotism", or the ones proper to a world citizenship, "those of cosmopolitanism"? And secondly, in the event of there being a conflict between the political community itself and loyalty to humanity as a whole, to which of these should fundamental loyalty be given?[37]

In theory an answer is not hard to find. Tribalisms, radical nationalisms and patriotisms, followers of the tradition of civic religions, would in both questions opt for local community, while the stoic, Christian, liberal and socialist traditions would cultivate cosmopolitanism, opting for universality, if it were necessary to choose between the specific and the universal.

---

[35] A. MacIntyre, *Is Patriotism a Virtue?*, The Lindley Lecture, University of Kansas, 1984.

[36] D. Heather, *Citizenship*, p. 246.

[37] M.C. Nussbaum, "Patriotism and Cosmopolitanism", in M.C. Nussbaum and J. Cohen (eds.), *For Love of Country. Debating the Limits of Patriotism*, Boston, Beacon Press, 1996.

It is plain to see that envisaging this approach in terms of a dilemma may seem fictitious. It may appear that in everyday life it is seldom necessary to choose between loyalty to the specific community and loyalty to the human "community". It is nevertheless true that it is possible to strengthen one of the two forms of citizenship (local or cosmopolitan) through education, treating the other as something secondary, as indeed occurs in many sectors of many countries, one of these being my own. In everyday life this results in a marked tendency towards appreciation of the local sphere or a tendency to appreciate cosmopolitanism, both leanings whose exaggeration does not enlighten without aberrations.

One of these aberrations would be the "*chauvinist localism*" of those who appreciate no other values than those of their own ethnic group, their town, their culture; another is that of the "*abstractionism*" of those who appeal to humanity as a whole and to universal rights whilst lacking sensitivity and responsibility for their own context. It is wise to avoid both extremes, and to find the happy medium it is important to analyse the reasons that might be furnished by those who stand for each of these options, apart from being extremely useful to bring to light problems affecting pluralist societies.[38] In certain countries, like ours, violent nationalisms or the rejection of immigrants are closely associated with a tribal education, blind to cosmopolitanism, ignorant of the fact that nothing human can be alien to us.

The great unresolved issue thus consists in educating in *a new wisdom*: in *knowing how to harmonise our own identities*, because each human being is characterised by a set of identities and only if one knows how to experience these harmoniously can one be a person, as Ortega would say, "in his right mind and vital efficiency". Non-harmonious personalities are disturbed and unfortunately, anything disturbed in turn disturbs others. We thus see the reasons claimed both by advocates of starting to educate in cosmopolitism and those of advocates of starting with patriotism, but pointing out right from the start that as I see it, only the balance of identities generates, in turn, persons living in their right minds and vital efficiency.

3. Educating in cosmopolitan citizenship

Cosmopolitanism in the west stems from an old and well-proven tradition, beginning in ancient stoicism in the fourth century before Christ. The stoics founded their conviction of being citizens of the world on two essential keys to their thinking.

---

[38] For this whole matter see the discussion between Nussbaum and the authors who participate in the book mentioned in the previous note.

The first of these referred to the truth that all human beings are identical, at least in one aspect, in that they are endowed with *lógos*, reason and speech, and are thus children of the universal *Lógos*. The stoic Cleanthes of Assos, invoking Zeus in his famous hymn, said "From thee was our begetting; ours alone of all that live and move upon the earth the lot to bear God's likeness".[39]

But precisely the identity of all human beings in being endowed with *lógos* and diversity in the other aspects gave rise to everyone's belonging to two communities, the local community and the community of all mankind, belonging to a political community, endowed with laws and consecrated to particular gods, and belonging to a universal community. The idea of this double belonging, by means of which we are citizens of a particular country and at the same time of the world, is reinforced in western traditions, thanks to Christianity which considers all human beings as being children of the same Father, and thanks also to such decisive philosophical proposals as that of Immanuel Kant, which secularise this Christian notion in the idea that all men can belong to the same moral community.

Indeed, Kant maintains that all human beings belong by birth to a political community, with which they have a moral duty undertaken, that of attempting to convert that community into a Constitutional State, where all citizens can exercise their autonomy. But each human being is also not only a *citizen* of a State, but also a *person*, able to be governed by his own laws, able to be the owner of herself. The human being, as a person, may form part of a moral community, governed by laws of virtue, able to design the outline of a Kingdom of Ends, a kingdom in which everyone is treated as an absolutely valuable being. As was seen in the previous chapter, the political community and moral community are not identified with each other, but mingle in together in such a way that any political community should aspire to build along with the others a perpetual peace between countries in which it is possible to develop a cosmopolitan way of being.

And it is precisely the fact of being a person that gives human beings a peculiar dignity, in virtue of which they cannot be exchanged for a price. The doctrine of the dignity of man here encounters a rational foundation, providing reasons to clarify little by little what people are worthy of, what rights they should be assured in justice through the simple fact of being people. This would be the rational foundation, ultimately, of a type of rights known as "human rights", that a certain Anglo Saxon tradition knows as "moral rights".

However, whoever considers it is essential to educate primarily in cosmopolitanism also understands that a person belongs first and foremost to the universal community. Those who defend this approach understand that being born in one place or another is *accidental* for a person, while what is *essential*

---

[39] Cleanthes of Assos, *Hymn*, v. 6, 7 and 8.

for this person, the *substantial* part, is belonging to the human race. Albert Einstein, when asked by a policeman to state his race as he crossed a frontier, is said to have answered: "human, of course". This appreciation is reinforced by realising that it is *impossible to establish an insurmountable limit between "us" and "you"*.

Indeed, if the citizen is identified with his or her fellow-citizens in being such ("us") and that very fact differentiates him or her from others ("you"), it is no less true to say that the limit can never be definitive, because that citizen finds a large number of essential dimensions in which he or she is identical to those who do not belong to their political community. In fact, he or she is identical in some essential dimension to all human beings, whether this be through the fact of being endowed with reason, enjoying autonomy, having a communicative capacity, having the ability to love, having the same genetic code. This identity destroys the myth of closed identities.

And with these considerations we find ourselves facing a matter that is widely debated in our times, the question of the *"differential fact"*. There are doubtlessly differences between human beings, but not just one, many and varied differences. People differ from each other through the political community to which they agree to belong, but also through sex, religion, age, cultural heritage and countless other dimensions, which form as a whole a personal being. Each of these identifies the person with the set of people who share it in the same sense (belonging to the same sex, community, faith etc.) and differentiates the person from those who have it in a different sense (belonging to another sex, community, faith, etc.).[40] But in any event, these differences are never such that they build an unsurpassable barrier between "us" and "you", as instead similarity through belonging to the human race is more radical than the differences.[41]

We are furthermore assured by some advocates of cosmopolitanism that blood bonds create a *moral obligation* of partiality, but not other bonds, such as political ones. Because in a good deal of western tradition we have been considering *impartiality* as the perspective which should be assumed by those who wish to formulate a moral judgement. To formulate a morally correct judgement, the proper standpoint cannot be that of one's own interest, and that is why it is important to find out if it would be acceptable standing in anyone's shoes, and not from the standpoint of a specific, inevitably partial person. This is what is put forward by the Kantian categorical imperative, but also the "impartial observer" of the utilitarian tradition, the Rawlsian "original position", the "rational preferrer" of certain traditions of rational decision, and even

---

[40] Ch. Taylor, M*ulticulturalism and "The Politics of Recognition"*, Princeton, Princeton University Press, 1992; I.M. Young, *Justice and the Politics of Difference*, Princeton University Press, 1990.

[41] A. Cortina, *Ciudadanos del mundo*, chapter VI.

to a certain extent the ideal situation of speech of the ethics of discourse. Though in the last case we are referring to a pragmatic counterfactual proposal of speech.[42]

However, there is a lively dispute between philosophers on this point, because some of them consider that there is a moral obligation to be partial in specific situations and in particular cases; for example, with people to whom we are linked by blood bonds. Indeed, if I can only give help to one of two people, and one of them belongs to my family, I have the moral obligation to be partial and help them; impartiality would in this case be immoral, on condition that this is not a situation framed in a legislation compelling one to impartiality, because in this case supporting the relative in spite of legislation would mean practising "family amoralism", which in fact makes the implementation of a Constitutional State impossible.

But to go back to the time prior to the Constitutional State, is the national or political bond one of the sort that morally obliges people to be partial and to help those of one's own national community rather than other human beings? Is there a moral obligation of partiality in this case?

Faced with a similar question the defender of cosmopolitanism replies that *political bonds* generate political obligations, but *no moral obligation of partiality*. This is why there is no reason to educate the child and the adolescent in the conviction that he or she has the moral duty to help his or her fellow-citizens first of all. One should thus educate them primarily in universality (not in particularity), in cosmopolitan citizenship (rather than in political citizenship).

And lastly, if any human being is recognised as such precisely through the recognition of other human beings as ""flesh of his flesh and bone of his bones", does it not prove impossible to put fences in the field? Is it not impossible to set limits on the community?

4.   Educating in patriotism

Those who advocate starting education with specifically political citizenship, to then go on to the cosmopolitan realm afterwards, also back this standpoint up with some very sound reasons. If we attempted to put these in order of importance, the first of them might be the point that has been made for some time now by Benjamin Barber, amongst others. Barber maintains that *those who do not wish to conform to the market and the State* will have to seek *sources of rooting in the warmth of concrete communities*. In actual fact, the *Gemeinschaft*

---

[42] K.-D. Apel, *Transformation der Philosophie*, Bd. II, Frankfurt, Suhrkamp, 1973.

that Tönnies talked about, the "community", and the neighbourhood, have been replaced by the *Gesellschaft*, by "society", and bureaucracy. It is no surprise that tribalisms anxious to entrench people in specific communities should emerge forcefully in a globalised universe: ultimately, globality and tribalism are two sides of the same coin, "Jihad versus MacWorld".[43] People do not want to be reduced to being treated as customers and consumers of a market and voters of a State — they wish to become members of communities.

In a politicised and contractualised world — other thinkers would say in the same sense —ethical substance wanes, which is why federalisms are healthy, because they allow different political communities to develop in a State which respects differences and allows them to survive.

Advocates of educating primarily in concern for the specific community go on to claim that universalism, when this is an *abstract universalism*, lacks sensitivity for differences and condemns heterogeneity, through being averse to diversity. This is why they do not understand how *religions* and *nationalisms* can still endure in the late 20th and early 21st centuries. The abstract universalist thinks that Modernity has clearly shown that the diverse religions are only appearances, phenomena of a single moral religion, of a single spirituality, accessible to the reason of all human beings. This common religion is gradually discovered with the progress made in the Enlightenment and rules out the need for different religions, held ultimately to be expressions of that universal religion.

According to the abstract universalist, nationalisms, which are inevitably particularist, should similarly have been washed away by the universalising tide of the modern State, through its ideals of liberty, equality and fraternity. Nationalism would ultimately be an untimely, outdated disorder, a pathology only explainable in times of disorientation.

In response to such affirmations of abstract universalism, blind to the richness of differences, those advocating educating in the local sphere remind us that both the religious sense and the feeling of belonging in specific national communities exist, and that it is better to channel these in a proper way to prevent them from degenerating into intolerant and even violent fundamentalisms. It is better to attempt to give concrete communities universalist values without depriving them of their identity than to attempt to dissolve them, a procedure that causes a spiral of violence in the medium and long term and which is above all unfair.

Nevertheless, I would like to point out that there is a great difference between nationalisms, that are essentially particularist, and religions. Religions, as Rousseau pointed out, can be at least of two types: citizens' religions and man's

---

[43] B. Barber, *Jihad versus MacWorld*, Times Books, 1995; "Constitutional Faith", in M.C. Nussbaum and J. Cohen (eds.), *For Love of Country. Debating the Limits of Patriotism*, Boston, Beacon Press, 1996; *A Place for Us*, New York, Hill and Wang, 1998.

religion.[44] Citizens' religions are the sort that internally unite each of the different political communities, and the gods of such religions are those of a community and struggle against the gods of the other communities to defend their own. These are the gods of Greece and Rome, each a god of its city. This was the type of religion that Machiavelli praised in his *Discourses*, because it identified citizens with their republic and invited them to become assimilated in this. Inventing "miracles", extraordinary events propitiated by the gods of the city is, as Machiavelli understands it, a morally advisable resource for any politician who wants his republic to flourish.

Christianity is nevertheless not a "citizens' religion", but a "religion of man", ("of the person", we would say today). It does not have the aim of bonding individuals together in the defence of their city, but that of placing each man in relation to the God of all men. Christianity tears down the limits of the city and opens up the frontiers to a universal religion, with which "far from leading the hearts of citizens to the State, releases them from this as from all things of the earth".[45] When Christianity has been used as a civil religion it has actually been instrumentalised, because its nature is not to act as leaven for the political community.

After making these statements, wholly true to the essence of Christianity, Rousseau proposes a deist-inspired civil religion, which he thinks is necessary to ensure the civility of the members of the political body. This is a civil religion, not a man's religion, because it does not have to commit hearts, but only behaviour patterns. Nobody can be obliged to believe in such a civil religion, but they are indeed required to behave in accordance with this, if they have publicly professed it, as it only guarantees that citizens assume feelings of sociability, without which it is impossible to be a good citizen; only this can guarantee the holiness of the social contract. Indeed, the dogmas of civil religion are the existence of a powerful, intelligent, well-meaning, farsighted and provident divinity, the life to come, the happiness of the righteous, punishment for the evil, the holiness of the social contract and of laws and the exclusion of intolerance.

Nevertheless, Christianity has no meaning if it does not commit hearts, apart from behaviour. Precisely the conversion of the heart, that Kant so accurately proffers as the key to personal and social transformation, constitutes the very core of religion. We can thus say that Christianity does not assure the holiness of the social contract, but the holiness of human life, and that of reciprocal recognition between human beings, which opens up the road to cosmopolitanism. Christianity cannot be a civil religion, in the sense of creating differentiating civic identities, precisely through its universalist character.

---

[44] J.J. Rousseau, *Du contrat social*, chap. VIII (Oeuvres complètes, Paris, Gallimard, 1964); S. Giner, *Ensayos civiles*, Barcelona, Peninsula, VII.

[45] J.J. Rousseau, *Du contrat social*, chap. VIII.

However, resorting to universalism can also involve the serious disadvantage of generating an undesirable and very widespread "*internal hypocrisy*". Internal hypocrisy consists in using the language of universal love as an alibi so as not to love concrete human beings, so as not to love our neighbours.[46] The language of human rights, discourses about the "North and South", solidarity with the far-flung needy are only too often smokescreens for hiding the fraud and corruption of everyday life.

Ortega's well-known affirmation "I am I and my circumstance, and if I fail to save the latter neither will I save myself" abounds in this meaning. The commitment with the surrounding world, with the social circumstance, is essential for genuine personal salvation.

Lastly, one should also add, in favour of starting education by the context close at hand, that the difficult thing today is not to convey an abstract feeling of universal solidarity, but to *construct loyalties in an atomised world*. When all is said and done, the ethical core of our societies, the ethic that is really embodied in these, is *hedonist individualism*.[47] Each individual feels that he or she and their desires constitute the centre of social life and that it is thus worth creating and maintaining links that lead towards that wellbeing.

This ultimately means the triumph of the individualism of beings who understand themselves not as people, not as individuals in a community, but as atoms each separate from one another, amongst which only instrumental links should be established. Our democracies are not so much of people as of atoms, persuaded that it is important to draw the maximum of pleasure and the minimum amount of pain possible from life. In this state of affairs, it is not difficult to use forceful sermons to hammer in a diffuse feeling of universal solidarity, an abstract indignation about the infringement of human rights; the difficult part is to generate loyalties to specific communities, to construct responsibilities for the immediate setting.

5. Deep-rooted cosmopolitanism

Hegel asserts that history gradually develops through moments, each of which considers only one side of any matter and is thus *unilateral*. From this the following moment emerges, which stresses the opposite side to the previous one and is similarly unilateral. But a third moment constitutes the truth of both, by taking the best of each and keeping it, producing a situa-

[46] S. Bok, "From parts to the Whole", in M.C. Nussbaum and J. Cohen (eds.), *For Love of Country*, 53.

[47] D. Bell, *The Cultural Contradictions of Capitalism*, New York, Basic Books, 1976; J. Conill, *El enigma del animal fantástico*, Madrid, Tecnos, 1990, particularly chapters I and IV.

tion that is qualitatively superior to the former two. And it is true that throughout history polemics between apparently irreconcilable doctrines have gradually generated other, new ones attempting to draw the best from these, reconciling them, that is, keeping the differences in a more comprehensive form.

In this chapter on the education in values of a citizenship bearing in mind the traditions of the Covenant, the Republic and the Contract, I should thus like to *propose* educating in a *deeply- rooted cosmopolitanism*, which attempts to embrace the best part of *abstract cosmopolitanism* and *deep-rooted particularism*.

Such a proposal attempts to assume the universalism of someone who knows and feels he is a "man and nothing human can be alien to him". There are thus no insurmountable barriers between persons, whether these be national, religious or linguistic. We talk *from* particular cultures and languages, but fully persuaded that we could make ourselves understood with anyone endowed with communicative competence, that is, with anyone, which is why it is impossible to trace out an insurmountable limit between "us" and "you" or "them". In this respect, the stoic tradition rightly marked out the path which would with different reasons be defended by Christianity, liberalism and socialism: people's *fundamental loyalty* is what they owe to people, as such.

Nevertheless, it is no less true to say that people are born in particular communities (in families, neighbouring communities, political communities) and throughout their lives join specific communities (religious communities, new families, new neighbourhoods). Ignoring people's community nature, believing that they are atoms separated by a void, leads to the perverse side of abstract cosmopolitanism, into which a self-styled Enlightenment has fallen only too often; to forgetting the particular contexts in which we work and to becoming lost in the world of verbal abstractions, of bureaucratic *lightweight* moralities,[48] which degenerate, as we said above, into "internal hypocrisy" and cause uprooting.

Why should one have roots? — asked a philosopher in the debate after a conference.[49] The reply is easy, in the light of the reasons already given: because those who do not learn concrete loyalties will find it hard to learn cosmopolitan ones. Fundamental loyalty is not the same as exclusive loyalty and "cosmopolitanism" is not constructed by doing without the specific "*poleis*", of the communities to which people belong, but from these; it is not constructed by eluding the differences, but assuming them.

---

[48] A. Cortina, *Hasta un pueblo de demonios*, Madrid, Taurus, 1998, chapter III.
[49] Given on the "Educar en la ciudadanía" course held in UIMP Valencia in 1999.

89

Obviously, building a cosmopolitanism deeply-rooted in concrete communities, which does not allow itself to be deceived by the vague ideals of abstract universalism, nor by the localist chauvinism of the closed communities, can only be done by implementing widespread changes in personal and social habits.

The *first nucleus* of discussion refers to the construction of the *personal identity* from belonging to different communities and different groups. One should remember at this point that a person is not identified only by his or her nationality or by the political community to which they belong, but also through a large number of dimensions which, when taken all together, make this person unique. But one should also remember that even a person's political identities, which form the person from the standpoint of political citizenship, are manifold, and moral maturity consists in knowing how to articulate these harmoniously, a process in which society must obviously be involved.

A person can at the same time be Valencian, Spanish, European and Western as regards culture, and a citizen of the world. It is clear that if one is in a setting that makes it difficult to live out one of these identities in peace, irritation proves inevitable. This is why it is important to find formulae which make it possible to live out the different identities of political citizenship harmoniously, to give the proper value to the fact of living with loyalty in each of the communities, whilst giving one's fundamental loyalty to the human community.

But secondly, and going from personal identity to that of *communities of different types*, it is true that we live in a fundamentally atomised world, in which it is urgent to revitalise and recreate *the communities of meaning*. Meaning, hopefulness, expectations are *extremely scarce resources*, which are not generated so much from States or from markets as much as from those communities in which human beings make their life more person- than customer-orientated, understanding the customer as being a purchaser or voter. We need the warmth of family, neighbourhood, religious, school, political communities, to gradually learn to sample in these the values that allow us to fit out life to make it habitable. Preaching weak values, disdaining the communities existing, is suicide, when precisely people require communities of meaning, in which to learn to live from strong values.

But these communities — and in this cosmopolitanism cannot be beaten, necessarily have to be *open* to all who wish to join them, and never closed, but *dynamic*, welcoming those who also want to belong to them, because only from open and dynamic communities is it possible to generate a real well-rooted cosmopolitanism. Without this it is impossible to stand up to societies impregnated with "moral republicanism".

90

6. Moral republicanism

Morally pluralist societies, ones in which there is not a single moral code, but several of these, inevitably come up against the problem of clarifying what persons or what institutions are legitimated to determine what is morally correct and incorrect in the different matters that affect their lives. As I have mentioned elsewhere, religions have different forms of magisterium, political communities place the capacity to promulgate laws into the hands of Parliament or other institutions, but in pluralist societies there is no Ethical Magisterium nor Ethical Parliament recognised by the whole social body. This inevitably leads to a certain "moral republicanism", meaning that it is the task of the citizens themselves to raise the moral standard of their societies, from their ability to judge and to act, from the different places that they occupy in society. Nobody can do this for them: they are the chief actors in the moral world.[50]

However, for shared life to work properly in republics, and in this case for the moral level of the society, it is important for citizens to have well-established virtues and propose common targets from mutual respect and from civic friendship. All of these things are impossible to achieve if it is not starting from education, starting from the beginning to educate genuine citizens, real moral subjects, willing to work well, think well and share action and thought with others.[51]

What are the central lines of this education, which is, as we will see, moral education in the broadest sense of the word? We will propose three, with the aim of opening up ways to joint action and reflection: the line which we shall call that of *"knowledge"*, the transmission of skills and knowledge to pursue any targets; the *"prudence"* necessary to lead a life of quality, if not a happy life; and *moral wisdom*, in the full sense of the word, which has two essential sides, justice and gratuity.

7. The society of knowledge

In theory, and in spite of the protests from some groups who complain that "educating" comes down to "training in skills and knowledge" in our societies, it is indeed true that education in both these facets is vital to have a "morally

---

[50] A. Cortina, *La ética de la sociedad civil*, Madrid, Anaya/Alauda, 1994; *Ciudadanos como protagonistas*, Barcelona, Galaxia Gutenberg/Círculo de Lectores, 1999; *Ciudadanos del mundo*, Madrid, Alianza, 1997.

[51] A.W. Musschenga, "Integrity — Personal, Moral and Professional", conference given on the "Educar en la ciudadanía" course held in UIMP Valencia in 1999 ("¿Son la integridad personal y la integridad moral objetivos de la educación cívica?", en A. Cortina and J. Conill (eds.), *Educar en la ciudadanía, Valencia, Alfonso el Magnánimo, 2001, 171-194).*

elevated", and not "demoralised" society. Not only because people with knowledge have a greater chance of getting on well in life, for things do not always actually turn out that way, but because a well-informed society has a *greater capacity to take advantage of its material resources* and is also *less permeable to deceit* than an ignorant society.

As Sen puts it so rightly, a society's income level is not directly connected with its level of welfare, because it might well happen, as it often does indeed, that societies with a low level of income but with a good cultural level have a higher level of welfare than others with a higher per capita income. Culture in a broader sense allows better use to be made of the resources available, which is why it is important to reinforce people's capacities to lead the type of life that they choose. In this respect, education in skills and knowledge, understood in a wide sense, is an essential factor in development, not only of people but also of peoples.[52]

Apart from this, and as regards the possibility of avoiding deceit, the citizens of a pluralist society cannot form a proper moral judgement on matters that they do not know if they do not get the right information. In biotechnological questions, economic problems, legal subtleties, in political readings, in the repercussions of the Internet for human life, in ecological dramas and in so many other extremely complex questions, having reliable information is vital for moral judgement. Otherwise only prejudices are in play, and though it is true that all human beings start from "praejudicia", prior judgements, and that the knowledge process consists in clarifying these until judgements can be made, it is no less true that when the process of clarification and information does not exist, only labels, slogans and not reflection remain.

This is why it is vital to have *professionals* and *experts*, sufficiently well-informed people, ready to place their knowledge at others' service. It is obvious that to do this, to place their knowledge at others' service, there will also have to be "good will", but similarly obvious that without knowledge, with pure will, a society does not grow humanly. In this respect, it would be better for our presumably "global" world if the anti-globalisation movements put forward morally desirable and technically feasible alternatives instead of simply demonstrating and rejecting what there is; that instead of saying "globalisation, no!", they should say "we want globalisation to go *this way and that way!*".

Proposing feasible alternatives is what is done by those who, from an elevated moral standard, place their knowledge at others' service, and make an effort to know precisely why they wish to serve. Ignorance will not lead to designing and getting under way a poor people's bank, a tax on circulation of

---

[52] A. Sen, *Development as Freedom*, New York, Knopf, 1999; E. Martínez, *Ética para el desarrollo de los pueblos*, Madrid, Trotta, 2000.

financial capitals, a basic citizens' income, international justice institutions, fair trade mechanisms, ethical investment funds, solidarity funds, research with mother cells, "relocation" of workers fired from companies, control of biotechnological research in developing countries. The lack of knowledge and skills is no basis from which to make a more human world, quite the opposite.

This is why we need experts in economy, in law, in business studies, and in humanities, in biology, in medicine, who are willing above all to do *three things*: to *design humanising and feasible alternatives in each of their fields*, and to attempt to put these into practice, to *present their proposals* to the Earth's power-wielders, in such a way that if the latter refuse to implement them, they have rejected a human and feasible option, and not an abstract affirmation; and to transfer their knowledge and opinions to the *sphere of public opinion*, to the sphere in which citizens of pluralist societies deliberate on what is fair and what is not fair.

In a "moral republic", in which the weight of public deliberation proves decisive, it is essential for professionals and experts to inform properly. But for this reason they have to have knowledge: attempting to obtain this is a moral duty. The acquisition process doubtlessly starts at school and in the family, but continues in universities and higher education, in this world whose meaning and legitimacy lie in training professionals, people with a profound knowledge of their subject, willing to be guided in practice by the values and targets which give meaning to their profession.[53]

Because, and here lies the second of our central themes, the amount of knowledge does not make us wise, just as the amount of products on the market does not make us happy. Amounts are always accumulations of things (techniques, goods), which need to be given a form to become fulfilling from the human standpoint. And "given a form" here means "giving oneself a good target", "pursuing a good end"; but clearly having sufficient resources with profound and updated knowledge.

8.   A quality life

Indeed, as Aristotle said only too rightly, someone who knows how to prepare poison to murder makes use of just as much skill as someone who uses it to cure, the poisoner being as skilled in this art as the physician. What makes technique good, and what makes knowledge good, is the good of the end pursued, and for determining the good of the relationship between the means and the ends he recommended the use of *prudence*. Centuries later Kant insisted on the fact

---

[53] A. Cortina y J. Conill (coord.), *Diez palabras clave en ética de las profesiones*, Estella, VD, 2000; A. Hortal, Ética General de las Profesiones, Desclée de Brouwer, Bilbao, 2002.

that prudence is a virtue required for steering skills towards a happy life, and that this is why children should be educated to be both technically skilful and to be prudent in the search for happiness.[54]

Nevertheless, though indeed valuable, prudence would seem to me to be too modest a virtue to aspire to such a radical condition as happiness. Kant understood by "happiness" the sum total of all the sensitive goods, which is why he thought it was an ideal of the imagination, and not of the reason. But it would perhaps be more appropriate to use the term *"wellbeing"* for the sum total of sensitive goods, for the goods which produce sensitive satisfaction, and to reserve the term "happiness" for a way of life in fullness, in which sensitive satisfactions are involved as ingredients, but not only these, since there are other forms of goods, which we will call those of "justice" and "gratuity".

In any event, the term wellbeing, or welfare, as used in expressions such as the "welfare state", "welfare measures", "welfarism", continues to be too confusing to be taken as a goal of the virtue of prudence, and we would perhaps do better to make this more specific in a concept as highly valued today as is *"quality of life"*, undoubtedly unattainable without the aforementioned virtue. Seeking a life of quality ultimately requires learning how to practise an art, that of paying careful attention to the vital context when drawing up projects and making decisions, pondering over the consequences of the different options that might be entailed for the subject him or herself, for their own families and friends, for any particular groups or for humanity in general, and ultimately being satisfied with *what is enough*. This is thus the state between excess and deficiency: the art of opting for moderation proper to the classical virtues, so closely linked with achieving a quality life.

We should remember that the term *"quality of life"* came into everyday use from the nineteen-fifties of the 20th century onwards, and took on a precise semantic connotation in the seventies, in close connection with Inglehart's famous distinction between "materialist" and "post-materialist"[55] values. In 1964 Lyndon B. Johnson made the expression emblematic when he stated that the aims of his policy could not be assessed in banking terms, but in terms of "quality of life". In his speech Johnson contrasted the "quality of our lives" with the "quantity of goods", in the sense that the former is gradually made material over time in a lifestyle that can be sustained moderately with reasonable wellbeing, in an intelligent life, willing to value the goods that do not belong to the sphere of indefinite consumption, but to serene enjoyment; human relations, physical exercise, cultural goods.

---

[54] I. Kant, *Grundlegung zur Metaphysik der Sitten*, chapter 2; *Pädagogik*, IX.
[55] R. Inglehart, *The Silent Revolution*, New Jersey, 1977.

Indeed, studies on the quality of life and on the yardsticks used to appraise this have multiplied since then, applied to such fields as the development of peoples or biomedical sciences.[56] One conclusion common to all of them in the realm concerning us now would be that quality depends on practising activities closely connected with the capacity for self-possession, the ability not to "alienate oneself", not to "expropriate oneself"; either by subjecting oneself to "extraordinary" means late in life, or by wasting one's everyday life in things that are not worth it, such as the quantity of goods or the unlimited lust for power, which prevent one from freely relating with other human beings.

Prudent persons, ones who "know what is good for them in life as a whole", attempt to keep a grip on the reins of their existences, not allowing themselves to be dazzled by the unlimited quantity of products or desires, which would end up enslaving them, opting instead for activities which are worthwhile in themselves, for the ones which produce freedom for that same reason. In this respect, an optimum exercise of prudence means preferring to have free time to use in human relations, in supportive and cultural activities, rather than opting for a disproportionate level of income; just as it is to opt for cities on a human scale and turn away from vast metropolises, to choose the loyal friend to an ambitious acquaintance, to take the path of cooperation rather than the course of conflict, to negotiate, and not choose confrontation when defeat is certain.

There doubtlessly need to be prudent citizens and governors who are similarly prudent in the different fields in which some govern and others are governed (political, academic, ecclesiastic, business and health sectors, and so on), for organising societies and also the republic of all human beings, going by the criteria of quality of life and not quantity of goods, of whatever kind these might be. Only this prudential vision gives meaning to the approach advocating the *sustainability* of natural and human resources, moderation in exploiting not only the resources of the ecosphere, but also the energies of human beings, which are all but infinite.

It is in this sense that educators help their pupils to settle conflicts with prudence, something which is also done by those who give negotiation courses at businesses or in public administration. Preferring the quiet life, the *aurea mediocritas*, the sustainable world to the hectic race is a symptom of well-educated intelligence, of prudence. What is now more doubtful is whether quality of life and happiness are one and the same thing.

---

[56] For the complex world of the quality of life see, amongst others, M.C. Nussbaum and A. Sen (eds.), *The Quality of Life*, Oxford, Clarendon Press, 1993.

9. The sense of justice and the sense of gratuity

Education in the search for quality of life is undoubtedly preferable to education in the search for the quantity of goods, but is nevertheless still insufficient
to educate a person in the full sense of the word, because whoever prudently
pursues a life of quality for themselves and their families or friends is not always
willing to comply with the demands of justice or willing to risk being happy.

As for the demands of justice, this kind of people take them into account as
long as they do not impair their wellbeing or welfare, or while they fortify this,
but if the quality of their life and the demands of those who sometimes do not
even have the basic goods for survival collide, prudence may advise excluding
these with no further thought.

We have had plenty of experience of this form of behaviour throughout history and we can still observe this in recent times, thinking for instance of what
is known as the "immigration phenomenon", which comes down to something
as simple as the fact that people in the developed countries are so concerned with
obtaining a quantity of market products and in the best case with quality of life
that they have no mental energy left over to worry about the profound distress of
"developing" countries, and even less volitive energy to attempt to help to create wealth in those countries. There may well be all the declarations on human
rights that you could wish for, but people who are actually educated to seek the
quantity of products and quality of their own lives are inevitably "exclusive",
excluding any who fail to come into the prudent calculation of their own welfare.

This is why educating people in the sense of justice always demands going
beyond calculation and prudence — not "going beyond" in a straight line, like
a road or a train line — but in depth, in interiority; pondering over what it is
that makes us persons, what it is that ultimately allows me to say "I", if this is
not the fact that others have recognised and still recognise me as a person and
as "you". This is the basic experience of reciprocal recognition, as told in the
book of *Genesis* —"this is now bone of my bones and flesh of my flesh"—
which opens up an intelligent human sense with two equally intelligent, equally
sentient facets: the *sense of justice* and the *sense of gratuity*.

The *sense of justice*, about which so much has been said and written, is what
constrains us to give each person what they are entitled to, and the issue that so
much has been said and written about is precisely the question of what pertains
to each person, this being the area covered in the different theories of justice that
have existed all over the world. But at this basic point, in this basic experience
of recognition, what is due to others and to me by right is what we deserve as
persons. So what do we deserve as persons?

Human history is said by Hegel to be the history of freedom; and our history
can in fact be seen as such. Nevertheless, I have proposed an interpretation that
is perhaps just as sound: telling this as the history of justice. Because over time

we have gradually loaded the dice of justice with demands unknown in previous ages. What is just is that everyone should have food, housing, clothing, education, care in times of vulnerability, freedom to express themselves, form their conscience and personally guide their own lives. What is just is that societies who wish to come up to the standard of minimum moral dignity should meet these basic needs or promote people's capacities so that they can satisfy them and lead a happy life. This theory of capacities is what is offered today by Sen, and one that involves the advantage over the needs-based theory of putting the authorship of their own good in the hands of subjects themselves, proposing the *"empowerment"* of the poor.

To go back to our own text, whoever recognises other human beings as blood of their blood and bone of their bones *demands* of themselves and *demands* of those who have power to do this, as a *requirement of justice*, that no human being should have the capacities which enable them to obtain these goods and pursue a happy life depleted. Such people use their talents and their knowledge, their "learning", to be able to discern all the means possible to do justice. Indeed, the names of these "goods of justice" are already to be found pervading Universal Declarations and International Charters, now belonging to the world of our "moral ideas", perfectly designed in the theory of discourses and books. But those who lack a sense of justice, who lack a just reason, will not turn these ideas into beliefs that govern their lives, not take them as the driving force behind their existence, but live instead from a standpoint of calculation and prudence in their everyday lives.

The sense of justice, both demanding and lucid, is a powerful driving force. It is largely "responsible" for the best part of our history, a history in which the goods that are mentioned above have been made material, made *demandable*.

But the fact is that the human world is not only one of demands and the demandable, and much less that of calculation and prudence; it is not only the world of recognised rights, with their corresponding duties and responsibilities. Whoever accepts the experience of reciprocal recognition, the experience of the Covenant with another human being who is bone of their own bones and flesh of their own flesh, does not only feel compelled to give the other "what they deserve" as a person, but feels bound to share with them what both of them need to be happy.

Happiness is a radical question, and goes right to the root, to that basic experience of those who are not satisfied with calculation and prudence, not even, and this is going much farther, satisfied with assuming responsibility for justice being done. It will meet these basic needs that can never be demanded as a right nor complied with as a duty.

Beyond right and duty, not in a straight line, like someone going along a road or a train line, but in depth, in interiority, the vast mystery of *ob-ligation* opens up, the remarkable discovery that we are indissolubly *bound* to each other, and thus *ob-liged*, even without external sanctions, and without external commands, but from somewhere deep inside. Saint Augustine wisely advises us: 'Do not go outward; return within yourself. In the inward man dwells truth'. It is deep inside that one discovers this profound bond, the secret of happiness, and from it flows the world of obligations that cannot be demanded, but shared graciously, the world of the present and the gift, of consolation in times of sadness, of support in times of distress, of hope when the horizon seems to have been blotted out, of meaningfulness against the experience of the absurd.

No-one will deny that to go about a decent life we all need food, clothing, housing and culture, free expression and conscience, but we also need — sometimes even more than these — consolation and hope, meaning and affection, the good of gratuity that can never be demanded as a right; which is shared by those who give it not through duty, but through the fullness of their hearts.

Educating for the 21st century will mean forming well-informed citizens, with good knowledge and also prudent as regards quantity and quality. But it will also, to a large extent, involve educating people with a profound sense of justice and a profound sense of grace.

V. Civic ethics:
between the covenant and the contract

9. SEMBLANCE OF CIVIC ETHICS

1. Moral pluralism and ethical pluralism

The development of the moral conscience in western societies has gradually been forming two now commonly accepted levels of reflection and language: *the morality of everyday life* and *ethics or moral philosophy*. Morality, or better said, the different moralities implemented in everyday life, attempt to give direct guidance for action, while ethics also guides conduct, but only indirectly, because its task consists in reflecting on the rational foundations of morality, foundations which are ultimately normative.

In the nineteen-seventies of the 20th century this distinction became quite notorious amongst moral philosophers, because they wished to find out if they had legitimacy to issue moral rules or if, on the other hand, only moralists had this, through citizens' recognising them as being legitimated to do so. It was said that there are ultimately different moralities with descriptive adjectives taken from everyday life (Christian, Islamic, Jewish morals, the morality associated with the different versions of Hinduism, Buddhism, Confucianism, etc.) and each of these is creditworthy for those who have accepted its principles, either through taking these as being revealed, or through trusting in the tradition which maintains them. What gives legitimacy to the guidance that moralists attempt to give are thus the sources from which this guidance comes, not so much their own personal lucidity or ingenuity. The task of ethical or moral philosophers would then consist not so much in giving rules for action, as they are unassisted in this endeavour by any superior power, but in attempting to elucidate what the moral phenomenon consists of and what rational foundations back this up to guide conduct. A great deal of the ethical reflection in the nineteen-seventies and eighties was concerned with arguments on the foundations of morality.

That was a time when certain ignoramuses rather curiously reached the strange conclusion that there are a diversity of moralities, but a single ethics, that there are moralities with different adjectives from everyday life appended to them and a single universal ethics. This is most evidently false, as is shown by the briefest look at the history of moral philosophy or the most superficial of interpretations of present-day ethical writings. Eudemonist, utilitarians, Kantians and pragmatists continue to argue about the foundations of ethics and about the possible application of such foundations, from which it stems that there is also a plurality of ethical theories, with descriptive adjectives from philosophical life. *The plurality of ethical theories goes along with the moral pluralism of everyday life.* What stance should we take in view of the plurality of moralities and the diversity of ethics?

The temptation of relativism or subjectivism is doubtlessly strong and a large number of the unwise have fallen into this, reaching the conclusion that there are no universalisable principles or values, but that the world of evaluations is always relative to traditions and cultures, or depends on subjective preferences. Nevertheless, relativism and subjectivism are low flying, short-sighted birds which are forced down to land as soon as they face the demands of reality. "Bioethics will save ethics" were the truly prophetic words of Stephen Toulmin.[1] Bioethics, the ethics of the economy and business, those of the communication media, politics and professions, have all saved ethics from the relativist and subjectivist illusion because social reality demanded answers on a human scale from them, answers entwined with universalisable principles and values. Because, without a claim to universality in values and moral principles, how can one establish if it is morally acceptable to research with embryos, clone human beings, let husbands mistreat their wives and children, allow discrimination on grounds of resources, race or sex, demand sustainable development or take into account future generations?

The universe of questions which open up before human beings in each sphere of social life is vast and the replies cannot come only from law, which requires long and complex technical proceedings to be positivised, but must also come from morality and ethics. From what morality and from what ethical theory? In the following discussion I should like to put forward only two suggestions: as far as the first question goes, from a civic morality, and as for the second, from a particular *ethics of discourse*, which is particular because it takes into account the axiological dimension of the supposedly procedural rationality, and because it proposes, if not a "theory of virtue", then indeed an anthroponomy,[2] but also because it embraces the contents of other ethical theories inside it,[3] and broadly recognises that at the time of foundation there is not only the logical tradition of recognition (Socratic), but also the experiential one of the Covenant, as we shall see in the next chapter.

2. Semblance of a civic ethics

As we said in the previous chapter, an ethical community necessarily takes universalist moral principles and values, such as justice, freedom or equality, which

---

[1] The title of Toulmin's article is: "How medicine saved the life of ethics".
[2] A. Cortina, *Ética sin moral*, chap. 7.
[3] A. Cortina, *Ética aplicada y democracia radical*, chaps. 10 and 11.

we would extend universally, as ultimate reference for its action. It is true that each political community has its own practices and customs, its particular nature (*êthos*), but similarly true that there are moral values and principals which are appealed to by the different groups in societies located, at least verbally, at the post-conventional moral level.

This assertion of universalist values and principles might seem to lead to intolerance in moral matters, because it consists in imposing certain moral convictions on the other citizens, and even on the citizens of different cultures. It is nevertheless quite the opposite: a society cannot be pluralist and tolerant if it does not have certain moral values and principles that different social groups consider to be unrenounceable, one of these being the value of tolerating those who think differently, or going even beyond this, the value of actively respecting them.

Hence it is important to clear up this point, by identifying three ways in which a society can live its moral values: *moral monism, moral polytheism* and *moral pluralism.*[4]

1) For a society to be *"morally monist"* means that it has a single moral code, that is, all citizens share the same moral conception, having the same ideals of a good life, and thus the same answers to the moral problems which they come up against.

   These societies are actually officially monist, at least if they are modern societies, because it proves practically impossible for all citizens in a political community to share the same notions of happiness.[5]

2) When qualifying a society as *"morally polytheist"* we are borrowing the expression from Max Weber, who spoke of "axiological polytheism" to describe one of the social results to which the modernisation process undergone by western societies leads.

   Axiological polytheism consists in believing that questions of moral values are "highly subjective", that in the sphere of values everyone chooses one hierarchy of values or other, but chooses this by a sort of faith. In fact, if they had to persuade another person of the superiority of the value hierarchy that they have chosen, they would be unable to provide arguments to persuade them, because such arguments do not exist; this is why there is a sort of polytheism in the field of values, which consists in each one "worshipping" his god, accepting its hierarchy of values, and it is impossible to find reasons able to lead us to an argued agreement, an intersubjective agreement.

---

[4] A. Cortina, "Civil Ethics and the Validity of Law", *Ethical Theory and Moral Practice*, vol. 9, n. 1 (2000), 39-55.

[5] J. Rawls, *Political Liberalism*, pp. 54-66.

It is true that in societies with a liberal democracy there is a very widespread conviction that moral questions are highly subjective and that pluralism consists in tolerating outside options, even though they may seem to be absolutely outlandish. Nevertheless, this would not be pluralism, but polytheism, and it is fortunately not the form of morality in force in societies with a liberal democracy or at least the form in force in the social conscience of what this should be.

3) *Moral pluralism,* unlike polytheism, demands at least a minimum of coincidence, not reached through agreements or negotiations, but arising from within, which is why it is incompatible with relativism, since relativism means that what is right or good depends on cultures or groups, while pluralism recognises common minima, valid for all. The values of which this common minimum is made up form the civic ethics which is the keystone for building the diverse professional ethics, and also the ethics of institutions and organisations.

This does not mean in the least that religions are dissolved in civic morality, and even less so the revealed religions (Christianity, Judaism, Islam), but each religion goes along with a moral approach in ways of life, and thus religious pluralism goes along with a moral pluralism. Bearing in mind that when talking of religious pluralism we are taking into account not only the difference between religions, but also agnosticism and atheism, the point is that groups with different moral proposals live together, some of whom resort expressly to God, while others do not do so. There is thus not a single "moral code", but a moral pluralism; but neither does "pluralism" mean "moral or axiological polytheism".

It ensues from all this that *civic ethics* is the set of values and rules shared by the members of a pluralist society, whatever their conceptions of a good life and their projects for a happy life might be.

People do indeed wish to be happy and be so through several dimensions: the family dimension, by means of which they are members of a family; the religious dimension, by means of which they are members of a community of believers; the professional dimension, by means of which they are members of a profession (teaching, medicine, engineering, etc.). Nevertheless, all of them are joined by the fact of being members of a society, a civic community, closely linked to other persons, who form part of other families, other believers' communities, other professions.

This is why civic ethics is an ethics of persons insofar as these are citizens, that is, members of a *"polis"*, of a *"civitas"*, of a social group that is not only religious, nor only family, nor state, but one that covers people's diverse dimensions (religious, family, professional, neighbourhood, etc.), agglutinates these and creates a bond between all of those who profess a different faith, belong to different families, work in different professions, share space with different

102

neighbours, but cannot make any claim to absorb all these dimensions of social life. One should always remember that the reduction of social dimensions, the reduction of plurality, kills life.

To outline the traits of civic ethics in my view, one should point out that this is characterised by the following aspects:

1) Civic ethics is a *social reality*, and not a philosophical construct, forming part of the everyday life proper to a pluralist society, because it consists of the values and principles that are already shared by the groups of that society which propose models of good life.

2) This is the type of ethics which *binds the persons insofar as they are citizens* and for this reason it can only be implemented in countries whose members are citizens, and not subjects or vassals.

   We thus accept the traditional distinction between "man" ("Mensch") or "the person", as we would say today, and the "citizen" ("Bürger"), understanding happiness to mean the target of people and justice the target of the citizen.

3) Civic ethics is *dynamic*. This is the *crystallisation of values shared* by different proposals of good life, which means that those shared values are gradually revealed over time and become more precise.

   In my opinion, the most fitting name for the different conceptions of good life is that of the "ethics of maxima", since each one of these proposes forming a hierarchy of goods able to provide a good life and also offers the foundations, the "main premises" of the reasoning by means of which one concludes that this is the best form of life. On the other hand, I propose calling civic ethics "ethics of minima", because this refers to principles and values shared by the ethics of máxima and by the political culture proper to Constitutional States, principles and values that cannot be broken without falling under minima of justice. The aim is not to distinguish between maximalism and minimalism, but to recognise the fact of pluralism and its characteristics.

4) Civic ethics is obviously a *public ethics*, but the *ethics of maxima are too* because, as we will see further on, *there is no private ethics*, nor "non-public" ethics — all ethics have the vocation of publicity, i.e. being made known to the public through public opinion, with understandable reasons acceptable by all citizens.

   Hence, the difference between civic ethics of minima and ethics of maxima does not consist in the former being implemented in the public sphere and the latter in the private sphere, nor lie in the fact that civic ethics demands public reasons and the ethics of maxima demands non-public reasons, but in the *way these oblige*; compliance with civic ethics can be morally demanded of society, though not imposed by external sanction; the ethics of maxima, on the other hand, cannot be a matter of exigency in a society, but of invitation. Those who are persuaded that a way of life is happiness-making have every right, in a truly pluralist society, to invite others to follow this, but never to demand its compliance, and even less to impose this by external constraint.

The sphere of civic ethics is thus that of justice, which is a domain of *exigency*, not only of *invitation* (ethics of maxima) but neither is it a domain of imposition or external coercion (law).

5) Civic ethics is an *ethics of citizens*, thus proper to the members of civil society, not a state ethics.

6) Civic ethics is a *secular ethics*, which does not commit itself to any particular religious confession, but neither does it set out to obliterate them.

Indeed, a civic ethics, which structures the moral principles and values shared by the different ethics of maxima in pluralist societies, *cannot be a confessional-religious ethics nor a confessional-laicist one either*.

A *religious ethics* is one which, as an essential reference for guiding our personal and community doings, expressly appeals to God, whether this be a transcendent or immanent God. A *secularist ethics* explicitly stands diametrically opposed from the believing ethics and considers it essential for the fulfilment of people, amongst other things, to remove the religious reference from their lives, extirpating religion, because in its opinion this cannot be anything other than a source of discrimination and moral degradation.

Both these ethical positions, assumed in a fundamentalist, acritical way, are intolerant with those who do not share their particular form of conceiving the good life. Taken as the ethics proper to the political community and civic community, they give some proposals for happy life priority over others, and thus constitute a source of discrimination in respect of the citizens who do not share the officially assumed ethical conception. This procedure generates the inevitable division between "first-class citizens" and "second-class citizens" and does not allow all of them to be treated as free and equal people.

In this domain it can thus be categorically affirmed that a civic ethics cannot be either religious or secularist, but can only be a secular ethics.

A *secular ethics* is one which, unlike the religious and secularist sort, makes no explicit reference to God either to take his word as a guide or to reject this. That is, it does not restrict ethics to the transcendent domain, but leaves this "open to religion", as José Luis Aranguren would say, but neither does it assert that there is no other foundation for morality than the religious one, leaving non-believers deprived of a rational foundation. Secular ethics is the sort that can be assumed by believers and non-believers alike, on condition that these are not religious fundamentalists or secularist fundamentalists.

Analysing what the relations between secular ethics and the ethics of maxima should be and what the procedure to bring shared minima out to light should be is a matter of the greatest urgency, because we are gambling a good deal of the future of pluralist societies and of society as a whole on this.

3. Ethics of minima and ethics of maxima: terms for everyday life

Properly structuring civic life and the ethics that put forward proposals for happiness, whether these be religious or not, is one of the urgent tasks in pluralist societies, and a good way to start to think of this structure consists in giving them a name.

In this respect I consider that the most fitting terms are the *"ethics of minima"* for civic ethics and *"ethics of maxima"* for ethics which make proposals for a happy life. These designations refer to the way of interpreting the phenomenon of pluralism which Rawls has been displaying above all since *Political Liberalism* (1993), but in my view they express the difference between civic ethics and the other ethics of a civil and political society more fittingly than the expressions used by Rawls. Rawls talks of the "moral conception of justice for the basic structure of society" to refer to what I call the "ethics of minima", and of "comprehensive doctrines of good" to mean what I call "ethics of maxima".

From my standpoint, the terms "ethics of minima" and "ethics of maxima" are more appropriate, first of all, because they are expressions which can be used in *everyday life*, and not only in the philosophical world. It is important to make use of these terms in daily life and for citizens to assume them as an unrenounceable part of a pluralist society, so they can never be duped by those who are prone to deceitfulness and have an opportunity to do so.

There is indeed a sort of "intersection" between the different conceptions of a good life, of a happy life, which cohabit in a pluralist society, which consists of the minima to which we referred above. That is, all these worldviews, all these conceptions of man as an integral person and his fulfilment in social life (whether these be philosophical or religious) overlap, and this overlapping means there is an intersection zone. Nevertheless, each group can provide foundations for these shared minima on different premises, proper to their conception of good life, their form of understanding what the meaning of life is, on religious or non-religious premises and maxims.

I consider that it is fitting to use the term *"ethics of maxima"* for these proposals which attempt to show how to be happy and what the meanings of life and death are, while the ethics of minima would not make statements on questions of happiness and the meaning of life and death, but on questions of justice, morally demandable of all citizens.

Civil ethics would thus contain the common elements of justice, under which a society cannot fall without at the same time falling *"under minima"* of morality. The "magic formula of pluralism" then consists in sharing minima of justice, gradually extendible, in actively respecting the maxima of happiness.

This does not mean, as is understood only too often, that the minima are a matter for the state, for the political community, and the maxima have to be restricted to a supposedly private life which forms the world of civil society.

And this is unfortunately a way of understanding the relationship between minima and maxima that not "those who should", but "those in whose interest it is" have taken great care to spread.

4. Public ethics of minima and public ethics of maxima

For some time now these have indeed been brought into fashion by people who would appear to benefit from talking of public morality and private morality, explaining the articulation that should exist between these one way or another.[6]

Whatever this form of articulation might be, the first problem posed by such a discourse is the one that says that two types of ethics cohabit in a pluralist society: a "*state ethics*", a political ethics which legitimates democratic institutions and strives to be made material in "juridical laws", becoming positive in these, and a set of "*private moralities*" which are the non-state ones, the non-political kind.

The latter are allowed to survive and coexist, but not to be presented in public, because "the public sphere" is identified with the state and political domains, with the area of coercion, universality and exigency. Morals not sustained by the State as its own should thus be relegated to private life. This terminology is nevertheless incorrect, and it leads to an equally incorrect conclusion; that in a pluralist society there has to be a *public-state ethics*, demandable of all citizens and on the other hand, that a set of private moralities, which should not be presented in public, is allowed to survive. This extremely frequently found conclusion is false.

It is so first of all because *civic ethics* is public, obviously and the State should respect and embody this, as it is the ethics proper to citizens and legitimates political institutions. But from the fact that this has to respect and embody such ethics, it does not in the least follow that this should be an ethics of the State. It is instead, as we have asserted, *an ethics of citizens*, a civic, but not State ethics.

And as far as the second part of the disjunction is concerned, it cannot be said that there are private moralities, but that *all morality is public*, to the extent that all of these have a vocation for publicity, the vocation for being publicly presented. This does not mean that they have a vocation of stateness, as indeed, neither does civic ethics. The different ethics of maxima, which are what tends to be considered "private moralities", precisely through being proposals for

---

[6] For this section and the following one too see also A. Cortina, *Hasta un pueblo de demonios*, chap. VII.

happiness for any person, have a vocation for publicity, though not stateness. This means that they have to be able to be expressed in public, and consequently that all morality is public and that there are no private moralities.

It is thus advisable to forget the erroneous distinction between public morality and private moralities and to replace this with the distinction that more accurately matches reality, between a *civic public ethics of minima* and *different public ethics of maxima*. All of them are thus public, none of them state, and both committed to the task of building a better society. What relationship can exist between them, and how can their forces be combined to form a more just and happy society?

5.   Time to add, not to subtract

It is a mistake to understand the relations between civic ethics and the ethics of maxima as being the kind proper to a zero sum game, in which some win what others lose. To succeed in implementing a pluralist society so as to grow morally instead of losing moral shape, the relationships between minima and maxima have to be those *of non zero sum games*, in which all players can win, on condition that they have sufficient moral intelligence to be able to see that what matters is creating a more human world, by combining efforts. Cooperative games, when the objective is a common one, are doubtlessly more morally intelligent than conflictive ones.

In this respect, endeavours such as the ones undertaken by the Parliament of World Religions are very productive, intending as they do to discover the moral elements common to all religions, transcendent or secular. Reinforcing these minima and extending them is the best way to avoid the conflict between civilisations forecast by Samuel P. Huntington, preventing the ethics of maxima from being used as weapons by spuriously interested parties.

Whilst on this matter I should like to put forward some proposals which could in my view make the relationship between civil ethics and ethics of maxima *a fair relationshiop* with the nature of things as they are, meant to bolster the moral character of societies, instead of weakening this.

1) *A non-absorption relationship.* In a morally pluralist society the ethics of maxima present their proposals for a good life and the citizens accept the invitation if they feel persuaded of this. This situation of freedom is the optimum one for making invitations to happiness, because those who accept them do not feel coerced by political power, as happens in the case of confessional countries, but neither do they do so moved by a diffuse sentiment of injustice in an openly laicist State. In a pluralist society the invitation and the offer are equally free, as is required by an option which is personal and non-transferable.

This is why the relationship between civic ethics and the ethics of maxima has to be at least a mutual relationship of non-absorption. No political or civic public power is legitimated to prohibit either expressly or covertly any proposals of maxima which respect the minima of justice included in civic ethics. But precisely because civil ethics presents its requirements of justice and the ethics of maxima have to respect these, no ethics of maxima should attempt to expressly or covertly absorb civil ethics, cancelling this out, because then it will install an intolerant moral monism.

Consequently civil ethics is not legitimated to attempt to cancel out any of the ethics of maxima which respect the minima of justice, and neither are the different ethics of maxima authorised to cancel out civil ethics. Intolerant monisms, whether these be laicist or religious, are always immoral.

2) *Minima are nurtured by maxima.* The non-absorption relationship only succeeds in allowing undisturbed cohabitation, not a genuine relationship of peaceful cooperative coexistence. And at this point one should remember that minima gain their sustenance from maxima, meaning that whoever brings demands of justice does so from a project of happiness, and this is why their foundations, their premises, belong to the sphere of maxima.

Underpinning these great projects, which are not something to be dogmatically defended, but willing to subject themselves to critical review, is one of the urgent tasks in pluralist societies. What is more, political powers should take advantage, in the best sense of the term, of the dynamic power of maxima, because politics is not only the art of eliminating problems, but above all that of attempting to settle them in such a way that the solution favours citizens' welfare.

3) *Maxima have to be purified from minima.* If civic minima are nourished on maxima and can find new suggestions of justice from these, it is none the less true that the ethics of maxima should often be self-interpreted and purified from minima.

In the case of Christianity, for example, the commandment to love entails making fair choices at least. A large number of Christians have understood such an obvious demand only too well and nevertheless many more, whether these be institutions or persons, have used the alibi of charity to excuse forgetting justice, as this is understood by a civic ethics. The memory of the Inquisition is paradigmatic in these cases, but there is no need to go back in time, because there are plenty of examples in our own age, in our own countries and in our own professions. In all these cases an appalling tendency is expressed: that of hostility to the demands of justice for causes presumably of a higher rank (love, State, group solidarity). This continues to be done by believers and non-believers in everyday life.

108

4) *Avoid separation.* If ethics of maxima and civil ethics draw apart, the dangers are clear. A *self-sufficient ethics of maxima*, alien to civil ethics, ends up identifying its god with any idol, whether this be its own selfish interest, or the nation, or the preservation of its privileges. On the other hand, *a self-sufficient civil ethics* separate from the ethics of maxima ends up becoming a state ethics, and the situation ends with man swallowed up by the citizen, or rather than the citizen, the Leviathan.

Reducing multiplicity, as long as inequalities are not created, is always unwise. The intelligent thing is on the other hand to optimise resources, in this case, by ensuring that happiness-making proposals are really ones of happiness, and that the demands of justice should be strengthened from their own standpoints and from the roots that give them a meaning. It is thus advisable to develop the world of revitalising narrations, to add, and not to subtract, and the bonds between the Covenant and the Contract should be tightened in this civic ethics which cannot be understood if either of the two are discarded.

10. A GLOBAL ETHICS OF CO-RESPONSIBILITY

1. The need for a global ethics

At the beginning of the Third Millennium the need for a universal ethics of responsibility for the human future is coming forward with increasing clarity. If in the *Transformation of Philosophy* (1973), Karl-Otto Apel called our attention to the need for universal ethics of co-responsibility for the consequences of technical progress, understood as a planetary macroethics, obligatory for human society as a whole, in year 2001 countless voices insisting on the need for a global ethics are being heard. Without this, *computer technology and financial globalisation* and technical progress will not be at the service of human progress, but will lead to a deepening abyss between poor and rich countries, and the diversity of cultures will end up in a conflict of civilisations, instead of propitiating a multicultural and cosmopolitan citizenship.

For the first time in human history we have sufficient resources to make the ancestral dream of a cosmopolitan citizenship come true, but to implement this successfully a global ethics becomes necessary. Such an ethics is thus a product of prime social necessity, and this is why so many voices can be heard reminding us that it is an urgent matter to construct "eine Globalethik", "une éthique planétaire", "a global ethics", "una ética global", to morally guide the globalisation process.

Nevertheless, the project of building a global ethics, with *normative power*, involves a great deal of problems. In theory, because relativism and contextualist pragmatism impregnate the atmosphere, in fact clipping the wings of any project with universal claims. Nevertheless, relativism and contextualist pragmatisms are themselves birds only capable of flying short distances, obliged to make a forced landing as soon as any of their representatives assures that an act, whatever this may be, is "unacceptable". If the infringement of human rights cannot be allowed, if the ablation of the clitoris must be considered as being a repugnant practice, this is because the West has ultimately recognised that assertions about what is just and what unjust formally claim universality, because there are beings that cannot be manipulated and things that are morally unconditioned. And whoever claims otherwise, from a contextualist pragmatism in Rorty's style, should attempt to lead their claims on to the ultimate consequences.

But secondly, building a global ethics proves particularly difficult in a world with such a diversity of cultural trappings. In such a world it is necessary to opt for *one of these three paths* when the outlines of a global ethics are designed: 1) taking a particular culture as a starting point and attempting to extend its ethical suppositions to the others; 2) detecting what the already shared values and ethical principles are in different cultures and constructing a global ethics from these; 3) taking an undeniable fact as a starting point and discovering by transcendental reflection a normative rational core which cannot be denied without being guilty of contradiction.

Considering the possibilities of each of these philosophical approaches for "providing grounds for" the normative force of a global ethics of responsibility is of vital importance and hence we will briefly analyse 1) the possibilities of the *hermeneutical-coherentist model*, proper to political liberalism, which takes the first path; 2) M. Walzer's model, that we could call of *"immanent social critique"*, which takes the second approach; and lastly, 3) *transcendental pragmatics*, cornerstone of the ethics of discourse, which opts for the last path.

2.   Three routes towards a global ethics

2.1. The *hermeneutical-coherentist* model, proper to Rawlsian political constructivism, ultimately attempts to "understand better", by means of concepts, the "fact" of the political culture of societies with a liberal democracy, which we can consider as being societies impregnated with a "reasonable pluralism". Precisely because the object of this is to "understand better", here we come up against a moment of the model which may be qualified as a hermeneutical moment. From this understanding we can attempt to build the principles of justice which we would like for our society, making use of the procedure of "reflective equilibrium", which consists in adjusting the concepts designed to understand our society (moral person, original position) with the principles of justice constructed and with the sense of justice of society, which recognises these as its own or not. This is a moment which we could describe with Hoerster as coherential.[7]

However, more recently political liberalism has also been attempting to build *a certain universal ethics*, to the extent to which Rawls, in "The Law of Peoples", attempts to apply the procedure of eluding differences between comprehensive doctrines of good on the international sphere, constructing something like a "moral conception of justice" extendible to non-liberal countries.[8] This moral conception can be taken as a certain universal ethics, which demands respect for fundamental rights and uses the *contractual* legal model as a resource to give binding force to moral contents.

As I see it, nevertheless, political liberalism proves insufficient to outline the traits of universal ethics mainly for two reasons:

1) Political constructivism enables us to "understand better" the "faktum" of the political culture of societies with a reasonable pluralism, and extend to a certain extent principles of justice tailored down to fit to other cultures, but *waiving moral constructivism* makes it impossible to provide foundations for moral obligation. From this it ensues firstly that only citizens who *in fact* have the sense of what is reasonable, as this is understood by political liberalism, will be willing to assume "political" virtues and secondly, that in the international sphere only cultures which have a reasonable sense of the liberal will feel obliged to respect such peoples' rights.

2) On the other hand, political liberalism would say that after formulating the requisites of reasonability in the international sphere, the question is to confirm that in an original position, covered with a "veil of ignorance", the representatives of well-ordered hierarchical systems would adopt the same peoples' rights as the representatives of liberal societies.

Nevertheless, one should remember that the metaphor of the contract is a modern western metaphor, taken from private law and led on to public law. It constitutes the sedimentation of comprehensive doctrines which interpret human beings as autonomous beings, with the ability to contract in the mercantile and in the political fields. But the ethical principles which give legitimacy to political contracts cannot be agreed on, because they constitute a premise of the contract itself: the moral obligation to comply with agreements stems from the reciprocal recognition of beings with an internal value.

---

[7] N. Hoerster, "John Rawls' Kohärenztheorie der Normenbegründung", in O. Höffe (Hg.), *Über John Rawls Theorie der Gerechtigkeit*, Frankfurt, Suhrkamp, 1977, pp. 57-76.

[8] J. Rawls, "The Law f Peoples", in S. Shute and S. Hurley (eds.), *On Human Rights*, New York, Basic Books, 1993; "The Law of Peoples", in *John Rawls. Collected Papers* (ed. by Samuel Freeman), Cambridge, Harvard University Press, 1999, pp. 529-564.

2.2. In this respect, a *hermeneutical-critical* procedure like the one proposed by Michel Walzer seems more promising than a hermeneutical-coherentist model like that of political liberalism.

Indeed, in *Thick and Thin* Walzer suggests a certain universal ethics which in turn respects the existence of a certain universal ideology and a "policy of difference", interpreting these in their strict sense.[9] To this end he introduces a distinction between "thick moralities", embodied in each particular society, and a "thin morality", able to spread beyond the frontiers, but only in critical cases. The thick and particular moralities contain a core of a universalist thin morality, that is presented independently whenever a social, personal or political crisis comes up. This thin morality makes it possible to provide a set of negative commandments which could extend to all societies.

It would thus seem possible to detect a *certain universal morality* which, remembering the tradition of the second Tablet of the Sinai, is expressed in negative commandments. The method used to discover this is socio-historical and hermeneutical, because the objective is to go deeper into thick moralities, and to find the thin morality in these marking out the bounds of what is tolerable. Nevertheless, in manifest contradiction with the presumed universalism already discussed, Walzer would say that from this thin morality we are not legitimated to criticise other thick moralities, but only to present criticism inside one's own thick morality itself and at most to repudiate the most brutal and offensive injustices.

We thus prolong the prophetic tradition of Israel, according to which, the prophet is such in his own land, except for Jonah, who was sent to Nineveh. The social critic inheriting this tradition measures his society by the ideals that this claims to have, which is why the criticism is *immanent*, because what gives it power are the ideals present in each society and not fulfilled in this.[10] Social criticism, Walzer would clearly say, "cannot work in a Universal Agency, but in a Domestic Agency".

In actual fact this immanent critical idealism is unable to combine universality and difference, because the socio-historical method can lead us to discover a common denominator, already accepted, and interpretable in a different way in each specific "ethos", which is not something to be taken lightly. But to be able to construct a universally coercing *universal ethics*, we will need to resort to a transcendental method reflecting on the unsurpassable premises of contracts and thin morality. The option must also be Jonah, and not only Elijah.

2.3. The *model of transcendental pragmatic* practises this reflection on a undeniable fact, the fact of argumentation, a standpoint from which the validity

---

[9] M. Walzer, *Thick and Thin*, Notre Dame/London, University of Notre Dame Press, 1994.
[10] M. Walzer, *Interpretation and Social Criticism*, Cambridge, Harvard University Press, 1987.

of contracts and the possibilities of thin morality are discussed. It is precisely the discovery of the unsurpassable premises of argumentation that lays the foundations for the *obligatory* nature of a universal ethics, coming forward as an ethics of responsibility, or better said, of an ethics of co-responsability for the consequences of collective action.[11] The meaning of this co-responsibility concept will be analysed in the following point.

3. The Principle of Co-responsibility

Transcendental reflection on the premises of argumentation results in a *fundamental ethical rule*, according to which, in Apel's own words, anyone who argues *seriously* has recognised that "All beings capable of linguistic communication must be recognised as persons, because they are virtual interlocutors in a discussion in all their acts and expressions, and the unlimited justification of thought cannot refuse to consider any interlocutor and any of their virtual contributions to the discussion".[12]

All beings endowed with communicative skills must thus be recognised as persons for our communicative acts to have any meaning, and this recognition is not in the least insignificant. In my view it constitutes the core of a normative ethics which deploys its effectiveness in the different spheres of social life, in which the framework of the different applied ethics is configured: bioethics, economical ethics and business ethics, GenEthics, ethics of the communication media, professional ethics.

However, as far as the present matter is concerned first and foremost, an analysis of the content of the fundamental rule reveals at least the following items:

1) The interlocutors' equal right to the justification of thought and participation in discussion is recognised. This equal right is an expression of a recognition of the person's autonomy, and the person should be invited, when affected by a rule being questioned, to express his or her interests through discourse and to opt for universalisable ones.

2) All those affected by the rule being questioned have an *equal right* to their interests being taken into account when the validity of the rule is being examined, even when these are only virtual interlocutors.

3) Anyone who *seriously* wishes to find out if the rule being questioned is right or not will have to be willing to cooperate in verifying its validity. This

---

[11] K.-O. Apel, "First Things First", in M. Kettner (Hg.), *Angewandte Ethik als Politikum*, Frankfurt, Suhrkamp, 2000, pp. 21-50; *Diskurs und Verantwortung. Das Problem des Übergangs zur postkonventionellen Moral*, Frankfurt, Suhrkamp, 1988.

[12] K.-O. Apel, *Transformation der Philosophie*, II, Frankfurt, Suhrkamp, 1973, p. 400.

entails assuming a triple commitment, which no competent speaker can assume alone and which thus requires *co-responsibility*:

(A) The commitment to ensure, along with others, the respect for pragmatic rights of possible interlocutors.

(B) The commitment to ensure, along with others, the respect for human rights or moral rights, without which it is impossible to practise pragmatic rights.

(C) The commitment to try and find, along with others, the most appropriate solutions for rights (A) and (B) to be respected.

(D) The commitment to attempt to promote, along with others, the institutions which best ensure respect for these rights. We should remember that, in my opinion, "pragmatic rights" are the ones that the interlocutors have to presuppose for each other on the pragmatic level for the discourse to have a meaning. Since practical discourse is the necessary prolongation of a communicative action, when the norm of action's claim to validity has been doubted, and since the communicative action is the mechanism for coordinating the other human actions tending to ends, we have to conclude that pragmatic rights are premises of the rationality of any act with meaning.

On the other hand, pragmatic rights in turn discover a type of rights, which ought to be described as "human", by following the steps of the logic of practical discourse. Bearing in mind that a norm for action can only be taken as being correct if all those affected by this have been able to give it their consent after a dialogue held in ideal conditions of rationality, it would be inevitable to respect a double type of rights: the ones referring to life and to basic freedoms, and also that type of rights without which there would be no fulfilment of the *télos* of the discourse, mutual understanding, whose configuration has to be made historically material. The *télos* of language is the agreement, and it proves impossible to attempt to *seriously* reach an agreement without providing those who participate in the discourse with a material and cultural standard of living which allows them to dialogue on an equal footing.

As we explained above, any factual consensus which might decide to infringe any of the rights mentioned would go against the very premises of the procedure by means of which the consensus has been reached, and the decision made would thus be unjust. And thus, the factual consensuses about specific human rights, which claim to be "legalised" in statements and constitutions, must respect the rights ideally presupposed and attempt to gradually make these specific historically, going by the circumstances in each case.

Returning to the central theme of our exposition, the point is that the commitment to protect pragmatic and human rights is an expression of a *responsibility*, which cannot be individually assumed, but which instead demands the creation of appropriate institutions to protect them. This is why we talk with Apel of a *Principle of Co-responsibility* which complements the individual principle of responsibility.[13]

4. Co-responsibility and recognition

Nevertheless, this co-responsibility actually emerges from a deeper source, that of reciprocal recognition between the present and virtual interlocutors in the discourse, as independent beings, equally legitimated to participate in the discourses. Only if reciprocal recognition, and not the *individual* nor the *community*, is the basic category of social life is there any sense in talking of a global ethics of co-responsibility. But this notion refers us to the discovery made by two human beings that there is a *ligatio* between them, which generates an *ob-ligatio,* a *tie* which generates *ob-ligation*. And this *ligatio* can be understood in at least two senses:
1) As a bond between the virtual participants in a dialogue, which is what leads us to Transcendental Pragmatics.
2) As a bond between human beings, who recognise each other as "flesh of the same flesh" and "bone of the same bone".

These two forms of bond are, as I see it, complementary, meaning that if the second of them is not recognised, then it proves difficult, if not impossible, for people to wish to dialogue *seriously*, and it proves difficult for them to become seriously interested in finding out if they are valid norms affecting human beings.

Indeed, the *first form of recognition* proceeds from the Socratic tradition, which uses dialogue as a cooperative procedure — as it were — to verify the truth of propositions and the correctness of rules. Transcendental Pragmatics prolongs this tradition and understands that anyone who embarks on a dialogue has recognised their interlocutor as being a valid interlocutor and must thus respect the rights of their interlocutors in a cooperative search for truth and correction, if the aim is to verify the truth of propositions or the justice of rules.

The *second form of recognition* proceeds from the tradition originating in *Genesis*. It is not now a matter of recognising the other as a valid interlocutor with whom I have certain obligations if I want to verify the validity of rules, but of recognising the other person as someone who to a certain extent belongs to me and to whom I belong, as someone who is flesh of my flesh and bone of my bones.

---

[13] K.-O. Apel, "First Things First", pp. 21-27.

It therefore does not matter if the relationship between the two is symmetrical or asymmetrical, it does not matter what rights or what duties may arise from the discovery of the tie joining us. What matters is for there to be that *ligatio* of mutual belonging between both parties from which an *ob-ligatio* going farther back than *duty* stems.

This is the tradition of the Covenant, which is complementary to the Socratic tradition and also lies at the origins of Transcendental Pragmatics, to the extent that this takes the category of reciprocal recognition as a central category of social life. Paying attention to this experiential side of reciprocal recognition is vital for a dialogical formation of the will of moral subjects, because without that experience it is difficult for a person to be *seriously* interested in finding out if the content of rules affecting beings with which no bond of belonging joins them is correct.[14]

The *"Gedankenlosigkeit"*, the absence of thought that Hannah Arendt identified with Evil, may stem from the inability to reach a level of thought higher than the conventional one, in Kohlberg's sense, but it may also come from the lack of interest in finding out if that norm affecting human beings is correct, simply because human beings are not of interest.

5. A paradoxical situation

Nevertheless, in the political sphere of liberal democracies a paradoxical situation comes about. Indeed, political communities with a form of democratic configuration submit to a Democratic Principle of legitimation of rules, as this is described by J. Habermas. The Principle of Democracy expresses the "performative sense of the praxis of self-determination of the members of a legal community, who recognise each other as free and equal members of an association which they have joined voluntarily".[15]

The Principle of Democracy thus refers to the attempt to solve the claim to validity of rules which must in theory be acceptable for the members of a legal community who have voluntarily agreed to join the political community or to remain in this. The political community is the one that proves most difficult to abandon for an individual, in spite of the growing phenomenon of emigration, and the legitimacy of norms can only proceed from the free will of individuals, as it cannot be sought in any divine origin.

This is thus in theory the specificity of the political world at the beginning of the Third Millennium. That in spite of the national State losing power in a

---

[14] For the notion of experiential reason see J. Conill, *El enigma del animal fantástico*, Madrid, Tecnos, 1991.

[15] J. Habermas, Faktizität und Geltung, p. 141.

globalising process, and in spite of tribalisms and nationalisms gaining strength, the basic political unit continues to be a community maintained by the agreement of the members of the political community. Transnational communities, like the European Union, still in the making, are also understood as being the result of a contract between citizens.

The specific aspect of the political world is thus that the notion of the pact appears as a legitimating source of legal-political norms, but this is a pact between members of the community, which has its roots in the doctrine that C. Taylor calls "atomism", because it affirms the pre-eminence of the individual and his rights in social life as opposed to any sense of belonging.

In my opinion, the empire of contractual rationality in the political life of democratic societies has turned our dialogical rationality into something strange in the political domain. This is why in spite of transcendental reflection revealing the bond between people, as valid interlocutors, as being an unsurpassable premise of the argumentation, the obligation to assume co-responsibility for the consequences of collective actions *needs to be proven*. This is why Apel's question: "Why should I assume co-responsibility? Is there any rational foundation for this?" is still completely meaningful, as well as Böhler's: "Why should one be moral?". In the political world the account of the contract has triumphed over that of co-responsibility based on reciprocal recognition. Why has this happened? I think this is because the model of the *contract* seems to be "*analytical*, insofar as it refers to volition", in a society whose basic premise is that the basic core of social life is the individual with his or her rights.

We should remember how Kant, in the *Fundamental Principles of the Metaphysics of Morals* gives two replies to the question "How can we conceive the obligation of the will which the imperative expresses?". In the case of hypothetical imperatives, "whoever wills the end wills also … the means in his power which are indispensably necessary thereto". This is why this proposition, Kant would say, is "*analytical*, insofar as it refers to volition", because the imperative draws the concept of action necessary to attain that end from the very concept of wanting that end. The concept of "will of a rational being" is analytically deployed in the sense that "he who wants the end wants the means", so no progress in practical knowledge is made.

We could add on our own account the fact that, applied to the political world, the rationality of hypothetical mandates can be expressed in different forms, depending on the situation. Whoever acts prudently can use conflict as a means to attain an end, when it seems most appropriate, or can use the contract, through understanding that cooperation may prove more fitting to attain the ends that are being pursued. In this sense, and through using the Kantian metaphor of *Perpetual Peace*, a people of stupid devils permanently opts for conflict, while a people of intelligent devils opts for the contract to form a political community, understood as a Constitutional State. In this case, the obligation of the mandates that have been agreed on by the contract seems to be analytical as regards wanting, because the individuals who seal the pact, seeking an end with this, must also want the means that lead to this. This is why they seem rationally responsible only for what has been undertaken, either expressly, or implicitly.

Nevertheless, to go back to the *Fundamental Principles of the Metaphysics of Morals*, in the case of the imperative of morality, it proves very difficult to discern its possibility, because it is a synthetic-practical a priori proposition, which does not analytically deduce wanting an action from another presupposed one, but immediately links this with the concept of the will of a rational being as something that is not contained in it. The categorical imperative entails an extension of practical wisdom, a synthesis, whose transcendental place has to be investigated by means of transcendental deduction, to elucidate the reasons for its obligatory power.

Applying these words to the political sphere of liberal democracies, we could say that the co-responsibility transcending conventions can be a real principle in different comprehensive doctrines of good, but does not belong to the core of unavoidable questions of basic justice, either within a political community or in the international sphere. The account of intelligent devils is what prevails in the political sphere to justify the legitimacy of democratic legality. This is why the obligation of co-responsibility proves strange *prima facie*. It is not analytical, but synthetic: it is added to the concept of will of a rational being, because the "will of a rational being" in the political sphere is, in the best of cases (in that of intelligent devils) contractual rationality. The narration of the contract has taken over the political world in liberal democracies, and others (the republican narration in the tradition of Aristotle and Hannah Arendt, the community one and the dialogical one) have *de facto* become marginal accounts. Marginal accounts doubtlessly have an influence, but do not occupy the centre. And reflection nevertheless reveals that the contract is not sufficient, but it is instead transcendental premises that give this sense and legitimacy.

This is why it is necessary to go on recounting the narration of reciprocal recognition, because without it, it is impossible to discover the *ligatio* which bonds human beings to others, and which is the source of the sense of *ob-ligatio* of some to others, the bond which is the source of solidarity.

VI. There is no shadow without a body.
Justice and gratuity

11. THE GOODS OF THE EARTH AND NECESSARY GRATUITY

1. The goods of the earth are social goods

Human beings love life and want to live, but want to *live well*. This is why
sometimes there are people who appear "to have it all" (social success, money,
appreciation) who one day commit suicide and non-one can understand why.
They wanted to live well but did not succeed.

But for everyone to live well, for life in all its fullness to become ubiquitous,
we urgently need to open up paths, break down walls, flatten out the steeper
tracks, bore through mountains and finally distribute those goods that are still
out of reach of all mankind, both women and men: the goods of the Earth.
What are these goods, and what are they like?

We shall start with the second part: the goods that we are going to talk about
are social goods. The people who benefit from them can do so because they live
in society and enjoy goods that would not exist in a solitary life, merely through
the fact of sharing life with others. From the type of food that they eat, seasoned
to suit their cultures and traditions, cultivated according to the country's technical progress and level of development, to the pleasure of reading a book or
surfing across the seas of the Internet — all these are social goods, socially
conceived, produced and even consumed. Because what people produce and
what they consume is the result of the work and the customs and practices of
their society.

This demonstrates the falsity of the ideology of "possessive individualism"
found at the heart of modern capitalism, according to which each man is the
owner of his own talents and capacities and the product of his talents and capacities, without owing anything to society for this.[1] Is there any human being who
has alone produced the goods which he or she enjoys, whether these be many
or few?

The story of Robinson Crusoe is not that of a "possessive individualist",
sole owner of the goods he produces, because he brings from his civilisation
all the knowledge that he applies on the legendary island, which is anyway not
as deserted as it might appear at first sight, but inhabited, and the best part of
the tale starts with the appearance of Friday. "I shall call you Friday because

---

[1] C.B. Macpherson, *The Political Theory of Possessive Individualism*, Oxford Clarendon Press,
1962.

that is the day on which we met" Robinson says to the native who comes out to meet him on the island. This is flesh of my flesh and bone of my bones. The history of *reciprocal recognition*, which had already started in the civilised world, the story of *Genesis*, of the beginnings of the human world.

Nobody is the sole owner of their capacities, because they would develop in an utterly different way if they had not been able to cultivate them in society. Will and ingenuity, feeling and reason would not even be those of that human "missing link" who already lived with other fellow-creatures. No-one is the sole owner of these socially developed faculties, nor of the goods which are passed down by inheritance. And this includes both family inheritance and political inheritance, for those born in the United States or Europe have no merit for claiming their own exclusive right to the tangible and intangible goods that they do not even dream about in Latin America, and much less so in Africa. The *"social lottery"* is a fact that does not legitimate those who are favoured with the best prizes to believe that what they have is theirs, because it is not. Although on many occasions they have applied their work, the prize as a whole was also the product of social effort.

The goods of the earth are thus social goods and should therefore be socially distributed. And not only in one country, but in humanity as a whole, which is ultimately what produces these; even more so in times of globalisation, when we can see that no-one does anything exclusively, that interdependence is the key to production and consumption, although people and countries continue to hang on to the false ideology of possessive individualism, continue to be persuaded that the products are theirs. This is why they dare to veto possible agreements which would favour the least well-off, because it is in their interests to make one believe that the goods of the earth are theirs (financial capitals, patents) that they have produced them and can do just what they want with their own belongings, without taking into account that we are all in debt to the excluded, if this is merely because they do not rise up to take what we have from us in both the local and world-wide spheres.

2. The plurality of goods

Nevertheless, for human beings to be able to live, and live well, it must be possible for these goods to be enjoyed by all those who are their legitimate owners. For at least three decades all those who are interested in ethics and political philosophy have thus been attempting to elucidate what the right *criteria* for fairly sharing out the goods are. Rawls started in his *Theory of Justice*, pointing to equity as a criterion for distribution and nevertheless, one better-informed thinker pinpointed the problem by indicating that there is no single criterion for establishing fair distributions, that there are diverse criteria and it is vital to find out what type of goods we are dealing with before determining what the fair criterion to distribute them is.[2] Clearly, when we talk of distribution we think of economic products, but these are not actually the only sort, and this blindness to the plurality of goods does not further justice when these are shared out, because some are forgotten, as if they did not exist, as if they were not vital to live well.

Walzer, on the other hand, enumerates twelve types of goods and devotes one of the chapters of his book *Spheres of Justice* to considering each of these. It might be useful to remember them and add a few more, thinking them over on our own account at the beginning of this Millennium, so as not to destroy most social wealth. These would be as follows:

Membership of a political community, as a citizen, *guest worker*, immigrant, political refugee, this being a crucial issue at the change of century, both through determining what it means to be a *citizen*, and what the immigrants' form of belonging is.[3]

Education, vital as we could say with Sen, to achieve an *equality of capacities*. To go on with Sen, the welfare of persons and peoples does not depend only, or even mainly, on the level of income, but also to a very large extent on the culture of the people who handle this income. Societies with a higher GDP have reached a lower level of welfare than others which, in spite of having a lower GDP, enjoyed a greater culture.[4]

Security and welfare, referring to the times when people are most vulnerable, when they are little girls, or old ladies, or sick or unemployed. And we should remember at this point, as far as our own country is concerned, that the privatisation of the health service and deterioration of state schooling can only lead to fostering extremely unjust inequalities: that the national welfare state can only be replaced by a *world system of justice*.

Money and commodities, whose possession a stupidly consumerist society identifies with happiness. "What makes us believe that the consumption of market products gives happiness?" is Scitovsky's wise question.[5]

Office and posts of responsibility, which have to be distributed going by the criterion of competition, as opposed to "familiarist amoralism", as well as demanding responsibilities.

---

[2] M. Walzer, *Spheres of Justice. A Defense of Pluralism and Equality*, New York, Basic Books, 1983.

[3] A. Cortina, *Ciudadanos del mundo*; J. Rubio, J.M. Rosales, M. Toscano, *Ciudadanía, nacionalismo y derechos humanos*, Madrid, Trotta, 2000.

[4] A. Sen, *Development as Freedom*, New York, Knopf, 1999.

[5] T. Scitovsky, *The Joyless Economy. An Inquiry into Human Satisfaction and Consumer Dissatisfaction*, Oxford,, Oxford University Press, 1976; A. Cortina, *Por una ética del consumo. La ciudadanía del consumidor en un mundo global*, Madrid, Taurus, 2002.

Hard work, which is not a good, but an evil, because no-one wants to go down a mine or collect the rubbish, if they can avoid it, which is why it would be advisable to perform these jobs on a rotary basis or to reward them with high wages.

Free time, so scanty in societies wholeheartedly devoted to work and gain and nevertheless increasingly valued by people as a vital step for a quality life. The quality of life does not depend on the quantity of market products, but on other goods, such as time available.

Political power which, to be fair, should be shared out according to democratic criteria of citizens' participation and practised with a view to common interest. Bearing in mind that the representative mechanism does not proceed from the democratic tradition, representatives should make a special effort to show with deeds that this is an inequality justified by achieving common good.[6]

Self-esteem, without which nobody can willingly exercise his or her capacities to lead a full life. This is why a society which wishes to be fair to a minimum extent is obliged to provide its people with the means necessary for them to be able to value themselves and confidently develop their plans for the future.

As Adam Smith once pointed out and Sen often repeats today, a society must fit out its members with the goods that allow them to "come forward in public without being ashamed". In Smith's England this would mean for example, wearing leather shoes, amongst other things, and in the Spain of the Third Millennium would be other goods, but what matters is that each society should know and feel itself in debt to its members as regards the goods which socially condition their self-esteem, not only on a local level, but on the cosmopolitan scale.

The *benefits of latest technologies*, which in a "globalised" universe cannot be left only in the hands of a small portion of humanity, even more so since all human beings and even future generations are affected by their consequences.

The *recognition* that some members give to others and which largely conditions self-esteem and self-respect. Being able to value one's own strengths is a basic good, without which no-one wishes to take on any vital project. But after going beyond that step, societies grant honours to some citizens for their merits, because they have made a special contribution to society's survival and improvement.

Equality, by means of which no-one should be able to have goods from these spheres with which they can buy all the others.

All these goods could be articulated in what we would call *conditions of freedom*, the conditions which a society is forced to promote for its members to be able to propose their projects of happiness. These conditions foster peoples' capacities to lead a happy life.

And now we have got this far we will make a halt even though there are still some social goods to be dealt with, as I would like to look at these in greater

---

[6] R. Dahl, *Democracy and its critics*, New Haven, Yale University Press, 1989.

detail, as well as the affirmation that equality demands that no-one should be able to use one good to purchase all the others.

As Walzer so rightly asserts, social equality demands that there should not be a *"dominant good"* in a society — neither money, political power, religious power nor the purity of blood should have free rein in a society to purchase all the other goods, because then some people would help themselves to all of them and exclude another set of people who would not be able to enjoy any. The latter, Walzer could have added- we would today call excluded and these are often whole countries.

There are examples of dominant goods in all societies. This position has been occupied by religious power, above all, in the ancient and medieval world, the nobility of blood in both these worlds, money and political power in modern societies and in all times. From one of these two positions it is possible to purchase the other and thence all the rest can be acquired: appearances in the gossip magazines, the possibility of obtaining literary awards, even of receiving some "honoris causa" doctorate, success in the romantic world, even special attention in the religious world. And with a little luck, as someone once mentioned light-heartedly, even the possibility of enjoying penitentiary work, if after enjoying so many goods it is finally discovered that the way these were acquired failed to abide by the law of the land.

Nevertheless, the problem is not here only of legality, but also of morality. Is a society just if in it having some goods means one can purchase the others, while some people cannot enjoy any of them? Clearly not, but what is obvious in words seems not to be in deeds, because in advanced societies economic and political power are dominant goods and act as such.

Lastly, there are *some goods* in reserve which we did not wish to look at until the end, because they are not normally considered the type of goods that a society should share out.

Amongst these there are *divine grace*, whose "distribution" is the task of religious institutions, their members and their officeholders. Churches, synagogues and mosques, Buddhist or Hindu meditation centres offer society what they consider to be a precious good, but so do priests, rabbis and experts in the *Koran*, masters of spiritual life. They too offer society something that they consider to be valuable and although there has to be a clear separation between them and the State, a pluralist society, which appreciates the diversity of goods, must offer the framework in which divine grace can also be distributed.

And there are also other goods in the local and global society, not often mentioned on the credit side of societies' balance sheets. There is *affection*, without which it is impossible to survive, the *meaning* of life and *hope, consolation* in times of sadness, *support* in situations of particular vulnerability. The dispensers of these goods are not political or economic power, but above all families, friends, neighbourhood communities, solidarity associations, religious associations. Why are these goods, so essential for human life, never seen on the lists given by diverse theories of justice?

Having reached this point we will now dare to put forward a hypothesis. In societies diverse goods should indeed be shared out, and the greater the diversity, the greater social wealth too. Monopolising any of the goods, excluding this from the "market" of supply and demand, means depriving citizens of a "product" which they could opt for if they knew of it.

Nevertheless, as we have attempted to show, the number of goods is much greater than the twelve proposed by Walzer, and it proves more appropriate for the real state of affairs to think first about what these are, and later on in what social sphere their distribution should be assumed. But what is more, the nature of each of the social goods is so different that it is not only necessary to think of different distribution criteria, of different "spheres of justice", but of the fact that some of them transcend the framework of what is just and what unjust, entering the broad path of gratuity.

As for the goods, there would thus be two large spheres on the credit side of societies, the *goods of justice* and the *goods of gratuity*. Understanding the nature of each of these and working for all human beings to be able to enjoy them is essential to really be able to open up paths to a full life.

This is ultimately the task of religions, that of opening up paths to full life, demanding justice for the unfairly treated from whomsoever is in charge of this, doing justice when those in charge turn deaf ears, giving freely what can only be given in grace. This does not mean claiming their exclusiveness because the realm of solidarity associations is fortunately growing, but indeed remembering that this is the meaning for which religions were born, the meaning by which it is important to go on telling their parables, the meaning without which they lose their flavour. "But if the salt have lost his savour, wherewith shall it be salted? It is thenceforth good for nothing, but to be cast out, and to be trodden under foot of men".

3.   Goods of justice and goods of gratuity

As has already been pointed out above, *"goods of justice"* are the kind that form what we call today a life with a minimum level of quality. Food, housing, clothing, work, civil and political liberty, social care at times of particular vulnerability, whatever may be needed not to feel ashamed in public, there are all the goods that citizens, merely through the fact of being citizens, have *every right* to demand in their political community. But not only that: they are the goods that any person, merely through the fact of being a person, has *every right* to demand of humanity.

124

We are not talking about gifts or favours now, but about the *demands of justice* which correspond to *duties that are similarly of justice*. We are not now referring to concessions, but to demandable *minima of justice*.

Obviously no-one can guarantee that whoever obtains these is going to find happiness, nor that they will fail to find this if they do not have them. Groups which lack what others consider to be essential goods have a good life, while some people who "have it all" are absolutely miserable. Nevertheless, though this is true from the standpoint of personal and even group achievements, it does not release societies from the duty of providing everyone on Earth with the goods that have already been considered basic necessities for the quality of life, such as income, housing, health care, security or education. Whatever a person does with them thereafter is doubtlessly their own option, but societies have the duty in justice to provide them with these, and anything else is downright cynicism.

Indeed, for this type of goods the political discourse, that had been interpreted in such a plastic way by the metaphor of the *contract,* woven by the liberal world is perfectly appropriate. As the parable of the social contract wished to convey, people have needs that they wish to satisfy and for this purpose they create the political community by means of an agreement, by means of which they give up acting according to their own appetites and thereby gain the advantage that the community considers itself obliged to meet those needs. The political community is legitimate only if it makes a real effort to meet those needs, which is why citizens are said to be *entitled* to have them satisfied.

But what is more, bearing in mind that each person is a member of the universal republic of humanity, each person is entitled to have those basic necessities satisfied. As Kant would say, the concept of cosmopolitan citizenship continues to be valid as a regulatory idea, which acts as a guide for action and as a criticism of the factual situations in which that citizenship is not respected as it deserves to be.

The political discourse of the Leviathan, though sweetened with the Kantian interpretation of the contract, is a good means of expression for stressing that people are legitimated in *demanding* the satisfaction of those *needs*, and so those needs become *rights* which others have the *duty* to protect, if they do not wish to lose their legitimacy, if they do not wish to fall into flagrant *injustice*. Because the world of goods that can be demanded with all authority is the world of the *goods of justice*, that have gradually been extended throughout history. Today these could be made material in the first three generations of human rights, and also in the notion of a cosmopolitan social and economic citizenship. Who is obliged to comply with those duties?

In theory, when a political community takes the form of "Constitutional social State" it is constitutionally committed to enabling all citizens to enjoy those goods, whether this is directly or indirectly. Discovering what the best mechanisms to get this are is a task pertaining to the political community in general, but very specially to governors, whose mission does not consist in gaining a position in the party, distributing privileges, thriving personally and as a group. Arbitrating decision-making processes through public deliberation, control mechanisms for representatives and procedures for demanding responsibilities is the work of the State and above all, of governments.

Political communities thus have the *duty of justice* to enable all their members to have the goods of justice that have been mentioned above and the key to their legitimacy lies precisely in seeking them. This is why citizens are *entitled* to demand such goods from them.

But not only do the political communities have this *duty in justice*, not only do its citizens have this *right*, but any person, through the fact of being a person, is entitled to the goods of justice and can claim them as such. Claim them from whom? At least, from all the societies that boast of having ratified the Universal Declaration of Human Rights of 1948.

As we have already shown, the goods that we have been mentioning are demandable from a *civic ethics*, that is not "minimalist", as some have thought or preferred to understand, but an ethics of minima of justice to the extent that failing to provide these goods implies falling under minima of morality. As civic ethics are expressed in different social spheres, goods of justice are the kind that imbue all social activities with a meaning: families should take care of their children, professionals must seek the good of their profession, public opinion must be able to be freely expressed, the economic sphere should create wealth for all human beings.

In all these spheres the groups whose roots lie in the experience of the covenant should be pioneers, as the groups whose existence has no other meaning than that of socially embodying the demands of reciprocal recognition: this is the extensive sphere of Solidarity Organisations, the extensive sphere of religions. Discovering situations of injustice and denouncing these and helping to do justice are tasks for such groups, though not only in universal declarations, but above all in specific situations, in daily life, in the institutions in which people work as professionals: at the hospital, the university, the school, the workshop; and not only referring to the past (Galileo, the Civil War), but above all to the present.

Criticising the injustices of the present time in everyday life is the great revolution still pending.

4.   Covenant and gratuity

Nevertheless, even though it means a great deal and is unrenounceable, this alone is not enough. There are a large number of goods without which life cannot be good and which involve the peculiarity that *no human being has a right* to them, *no-one can claim them in strict justice*.

No-one is entitled to be consoled when sadness comes.

- *My* son has died and he was the person I loved most in the world.
- I'm very sorry — the civil servant will say —, fill in the form and we will tell you when your turn comes round.
- How long will it take to notify me?
- At least a couple of months, there is a very long waiting list.
- But I need consolation *now*. And I pay my taxes, you know!

No-one can demand hope, if they no longer hope for anything.

And at the other end of the line there cannot be only a psychologist mastering persuasion techniques, as if everyone were stupid, downright stupid. Because someone who has no hope cannot give this either.

No-one can demand that someone else should infuse them with hopefulness.

"Children today just don't have enthusiasm for anything" — say some bored adults, from the 68 generation with imagination that goes no further than talk about expensive wines, exquisite meals or dream homes.
If at least they had sold their soul to the devil for the love of Margaret, things might have been funnier!
The devil is mystery, and Margaret is love.
But selling one's soul to the vulgarity of consumer society and then repeating the "bureaucratic *diet* morality", condemning exclusion and racism, the defence of human rights…![7]
And they wonder why they do not convey enthusiasm, indeed.

No-one can claim a meaning for their lives at a counter.

Javier Gafo was going to visit Ramón Sampedro and tell him that life can have a meaning even in those conditions of suffering. But Ramón could not see any, and asked for them to help him die.

No-one is entitled to be loved when they are hurt by loneliness.

Diego Gracia says that at a hospital a patient asked for help to die, because the quality of his life seemed worse than death. But it turned out that he fell in love with a nurse and no longer wanted to die.
Most people would smile at the story, but the smile freezes on their faces when they are asked: do nurses thus have the duty to make patients who do not wish to go on living fall in love?

No-one is entitled to trust that the end of the tale will not be the most resounding failure or the most unsubstantial banality.

---

[7] A. Cortina, *Hasta un pueblo de demonios*, chap. III.

Because the end of the story may be an "*optimum*", but in view of how the human race behaves (war, famine, destruction of the ecosphere) it has every likelihood of being a "*pessimum*".

These and other similar goods are not benefits to which people "are entitled" and which others have "the duty" to provide and nevertheless, they are *needs* that people have, to be able to lead a good life, they are needs that can only be met through others; through others who have discovered, not the *duty of justice*, but the *gracious ob-ligation* to have one's eyes wide open to suffering.

The point is that not all human needs required to lead a good life can or ever will be able to be protected with a right. It is true, as we have seen, that the satisfaction of many of these needs has for a long time been considered as being the object of an "imperfect duty of beneficence" and not as the object of a "perfect duty in justice". It is also true that the story of the West can be interpreted, as we have done in this work, as the gradual conversion of the duties of beneficence into duties of justice, like the development of the Idea of Justice. But we are not now talking of these two types of duties and rights, but of something quite different. We are talking of the difference existing between a sort of needs that can become duties and whose satisfaction can thus be demanded in justice, and other needs that *can never be demanded in justice*, because they can only be met from *the fullness of heart*. This is why we call them not "of beneficence" but "of gratuity": because they can never be the object of a *contract*, and can only be born of a *covenant*.

In 1885 French philosopher Jean Marie Guyau published a book with the beautiful title *Sketch of a morality with no obligation nor sanction*. In this he referred to Saint Augustine's famous invitation, "Love, and do what you will", both actually connected with the morality of the Nietzschean superman, who lives from superabundance, beyond any obligation and sanction, as Jesús Conill points out in *El poder de la mentira*. In both cases the terms "obligation" and "sanction" are loaded with gloomy connotations from the world of commands and instructions, to which people retort "and why should I?".

Nevertheless, and without denying the beauty of either of these proposals, we ought perhaps to take the drama out of the term "obligation". The word "ob-ligatio" refers, more than mandates, to the fact of people being necessarily linked, either to *reality*, from which they cannot be "detached", to *other persons,* to the *community* in which they live, to the *humanity* of which they form part, or to a *God*, to whom they are bonded as ultimate foundation of their existence.[8] This is why the obligation represents an unavoidable way of being a person, to such an extent that whoever does not feel bonded to anything or anyone, instead of being supremely free, is utterly unhappy.

---

[8] X. Zubiri, *El hombre y Dios*, Madrid, Alianza, 1984.

Freedom does not set out so much to destroy all links, all bonds, as to discern which of these enslave and which on the other hand reinforce a person's very being himself. Human freedom is never *ab-solute*, free from everything, disconnected from everything, but *ob-liged*, linked to persons and the things that are part of myself, which are valuable in themselves and for this reason go beyond any price, beyond any calculation.

At the end of a new bridge, Heinrich Böll tells us, the building company built a hut for an employee to count the number of people crossing it. With the data obtained experts would make their multiplications and divisions, work out percentages and give forecasts. With scrupulous punctuality the employee does his counting job, except for two times of day, when his lover crosses the bridge to go to work and go back home, because he does not wish to see her counted, quantified, converted into a number which is multiplied and divided, acting as a base for formulating percentages and forecasts. Because for him she is "the Unquantified beloved one", "Die ungezählte Geliebte".

For the point is that full life, which flows through the veins of human beings, is an immense objection of the conscience to quantification, an amendment to percentages, a continuous disobedience to forecasts, ultimately a commitment to what has value and it is unwise to give it a price.

This is why there is an *"ob-ligation"* deeper than duty, although unfortunately we have been educated in the culture of duty. There is an "ob-ligation" which is born when we discover that we are *linked* to each other and for this reason we are mutually ob-liged, that the others are for us "bone of our bones and blood of our blood" and this is why our life cannot be good if we do not share tenderness and consolation, hope and meaning with others.

This is the discovery of that *mysterious bond* that leads to sharing what cannot be demanded as a right nor given as a duty, because it comes into the ample domain of *gratuity*.

12. THE FUTURE OF CHRISTIANITY

1. Proactive, not reactive religion

As a new millennium starts, in this case the third since Christ's birth, it is not strange that there are often questions about the future of certain fields of wisdom ("the future of philosophy", "the future of theology") and of certain causes ("the future of solidarity", "the future of socialism"): the future precisely of those wisdoms and causes which seem to be missing the train of history and being left at the wayside, because when we ask about the future we are more interested in whether they have one at all than concerned with a verbal tense — whether or not these are "competitive" wisdoms and causes, to express this in business language, ones that may be supposed to be feasible in the future and which will generate new "customers".

It nevertheless just so happens that these very questions plainly reveal the nature of the present day, rather than times to come (of which we know nothing), because few would ask about the future of religion or theology in the time of Christ or in the Middle Ages, while today no-one questions that of the economy, political power, law or technology. Could there be any more stupid question than one that casts doubt on the feasibility of these social activities? Not many questions are likely to be asked anyway, because asking oneself only has any meaning with fields that are apparently in a crisis situation.

Crises —we ought to remember — are seldom universal, and in countries such as the Islamic ones and a large number of Latin American states, to use obvious examples, there is no meaning in asking about the feasibility of religion. This usually happens in western societies with a liberal democracy, and above all in European states, in which there is a combination of *at least three factors*, as I see it decisive, that we will gradually look into throughout this chapter, to make *proactive, not reactive proposals* from these standpoints.

The wisdom and activities which perish with crises are the reactive ones, that drag along at the back in the train of history, the ones with no reflexes apart from reacting against social changes late and badly. The ones that survive and invigorate human life, on the other hand, are those that *anticipate the future, creating this*, the ones that imagine what might be the best for human beings and design this, the ones that do not repeat the same old stories, but launch their message from the future.

Crises, apart from not being universal, are *constants in mankind's history*, because they are linked to social change and there is no society which does not change and need to adapt its body to new situations. These periods of adaptation are periods of crisis, in which it is decided if some parts of society continue to be essential for human life, but in a modified form to face up to new situations or if these are instead a dead weight which only now stifles social life.

The solution to the crisis can thus be either the growth of the social item in question or its "social death", which does not come with that sort of fatalism of which the comfortable and inert sort are so fond, quite satisfied with their "nothing can be done", "that's the way things are", but has instead a lot to do with what has been called "the prophecy which fulfils itself". In human things, in which freedom is involved, prophesying what is going to occur often goes along with making an effort for this to occur, so that there is a lot more Pelagianism than Jansenism here, more anticipation than reaction. "Let the Lord build us the house" indeed, but let us see if we cannot design the plans and contract the architects and workmen. They will get tired in vain, but what does that matter!

130

2. Normalising the religious fact: complex citizenship

One of the reasons why Christianity is in a crisis situation in certain western societies is that the issue of religion is as vital as it is prohibited in these: it is not only out of fashion, but "socially incorrect". If it is not to attack the churches or their hierarchies, it is practically obscene to talk of religion in media that are not avowedly religious, and sometimes even in these, and it does not cease to be curious that in societies tired of talking about tolerance and pluralism the believer has to practise self-censorship if he does not wish to be excluded from the book of those who are entitled to existence.

It tends to be said that the blame for this effective exclusion is the churches' and the hierarchies', for having allied with political and economic powers and done so much damage. The truth is that this has often been the case, but it is also true that for centuries there have also been all those others, who have given and still give their lives through that religious experience which is not only that of love for God, but the experience of love for others, in such a way that proves impossible to separate them. This can be heard on the news, when they announce that all the foreigners have abandoned a country at war, except for the missionaries, men and women with a vital commitment to a people whom they do not wish to abandon. This is proved by the everyday life of those who have openly given up their lives for a conviction of religious faith, made of both love for God and commitment to others.

This is why I feel that it reveals a radical hypocrisy in these supposedly pluralist and tolerant societies that such people cannot quietly express their religious affinity, when everyone is allowed, as they should be indeed, to express national, sexual or football preferences. To be a supporter of the Atlético de Madrid team is perfectly respectable, and far more so to be one of Barça or Real Madrid, which is almost the hallmark of glory. To be a Valencia fan, you have to be as brave as a lion, and I only mention that because Valencia is my part of the world. But to be a believer is a synonym of being a "moron" and "antisocial" and this is why people "privatise" their belief, and hold their tongues about it. This is not only an unjust situation, but closely linked with the future of Christianity in my way of thinking.

In these societies, as we have already mentioned, politics must be secular, not secularist nor confessional; it must allow religions that comply with the minimum ethics required to grow, without being committed to any of these, because that would generate second-class citizens (non-believers) nor eliminating any religion either, because that would generate second-class citizens (believers). But taking laicity seriously in pluralist societies would seem to be an enormously difficult task.

Believers do not seem to take religion very seriously because, as Nietzsche said, they do not look precisely as if they have been saved; the ones who preach civic ethics display the most elementary egoism in everyday life, and the tolerant ones only tolerate those who can give them some help when they need this. It is thus not strange that young people, to whom all these discourses seem strange at first, end up joining the ranks of the pragmatists, the only sect which would appear to have practising believers. Perhaps young people actually continue to value vital consistency.

Nevertheless, as we said, in these matters involving human freedom the prophecy which fulfils itself continues to be the best premonition, and the future of Christianity, as far as people are concerned, depends to a large extent on the believers really believing that they have in their hands something highly valuable for personal and shared life, whatever may be done by the hierarchies, which is ultimately a secondary matter.

And it also depends to a large extent on belonging to a believers' community being considered something quite normal, as one of the communities that form what has been called "differentiated citizenship" or "complex citizenship". If complex citizenship is the sort which does not ignore differences, but embraces differences such as the sexual or linguistic sort, it will similarly have to accept religious differences and recognise that this is a form of identity at least as respectable as others. And not only because anything else is discrimination and unjust exclusion, but because if the religious identity is not recognised as something normal, the story that may be recounted by the believer is discredited before it starts.

3. Dying of success

The second reason why Christianity is in a state of crisis in Europe is because it seems to be dying of success. A good deal of its messages have become such an intrinsic part of the different communities' moral and political life that they seem to have become superfluous.

In the same way as Machiavelli advised Lorenzo de Médicis in *The Prince* to use every effort to make himself superfluous, to succeed in ensuring peace to such a point that citizens could go on governing the republic by themselves, through joint deliberation and civic virtue, Christianity (along with other inspirations) could be thought to have fecundated western morality and politics to such an extent that it would seem to have exhausted all its discourse in these.

In this respect the "secularisation process" would mean that what was considered to be revealed truth is kept in the "secular world" and goes on having force for guiding human action, only that now its normative force does not rest on God's authority, but on human reason's capacity to give guidance. And indeed when we remember the *central traits* of civic ethics we realise that all of these come from religious accounts from the Jewish and Christian tradition, which is why there is such a proximity between civic ethics and believers' morality. But we also realise that in each of these there is something that reason cannot completely take charge of, because it depends on the account of the covenant of human beings with each other and of God with them.

1) The first religious root of civic ethics would be precisely the recognition of the *holiness* of the person, which takes on secular form in the idea of *dignity*, a basis commonly accepted in human rights.

    Nevertheless, precisely through having its roots in the idea of the holiness of the person, made in God's image and likeness, dignity mysteriously extends not only to persons able to set themselves laws, as the Kantian foundation of morals would imply, but instead to all those who are born of woman, even in the case of those who have no sign of ever being able to self-legislate.[9] The mystery thus forms part of the very core of human dignity and it does not prove a simple matter to discard the mysterious roots.[10]

2) The *reciprocal recognition* of those who feel flesh of the same flesh and bone of the same bones fosters these *duties of justice*, which urgently demand satisfying needs converted into *rights*, and opens up the road of dialogue and of the need for a political organisation acting deliberatively, taking advantage of communicative potential, which should be the real power of shared life.

    But to go even further, reciprocal recognition leads people to the obligation of the covenant, to the broad field of the *gratuity* of whoever feels obliged through fullness of heart; to the broad field of grace and the gift, which emerge from the account of *Genesis*, but even more so from John's Gospel. Because the Law was given by Moses, but grace and truth came by Jesus Christ.

3) The third key, the *community one,* also has its roots in a Christian tradition, and not only Aristotelian, because it takes from Christianity its trust in the spirit becoming present in the *community*.

    The spirit, Hegel would say, is what transcends solitary self-consciousness, and this is why we talk in the everyday language of the spirit of a people, of an age, which is unfolded in history. The *Spirit of God*, in Christian tradition, becomes present in the *community* and this is why the community is essential, not only to survive, but also to guide one's own conduct towards justice and happiness.

4) But precisely through it being that Spirit — the Spirit of God — which encourages the community of all human beings, the Kantian Kingdom of

---

[9] Adela Cortina, *Ética mínima*, chap. 10.

[10] See, amongst others, J.I. González Faus, *Proyecto de hermano. Visión creyente del hombre*, Santander, Sal Terrae (2nd ed.), 1991; J.L. Ruiz de la Peña, *Imagen de Dios*, Santander, Sal Terrae, 1988; *El don de Dios*, Santander, Sal Terrae, 1991.

Ends and the Marxian ideal of a world of freely associated producers governing the economy autonomously have their roots in this *community of all those who can be hearers of the word*, in this "New Humanity",[11] in what the discursive ethics call the ideal community of communication, which includes all those who are really or virtually endowed with communicative skill.

The difference here lies in the fact that these ideal and utopian communities do not even claim to wipe away one's tears, put an end to suffering, overcome illness, conquer death, which is what forms to such a large extent the core of Christianity.[12]

The ethical discourse of dignity and dialogue, of the local and cosmopolitan community, of the equality and freedom of all human beings does not set out to absorb all the blood of the Christian religion, draining this of content through a secularisation process, by means of which the great Christian messages would issue out into the "secular world" lock stock and barrel, and then no longer leave any space for religion; first of all, because the religious roots of civic ethics offer and ask for a lot more than its secularised version, pointing to maxima of full life. But also because those maxima cast a shadow on the minima of justice, which, as Nietzsche so clearly saw, *is the shadow of the Christian God*.

At the present time the requirements of justice and the invitations to happiness coexist, entwined together, and the shadow remains even though the body is concealed. But what would happen if it were not only hidden, but disappeared? What would happen with the values living in the shadow if there were really no body?

It would not seem that Christianity is going to emerge from the crisis by dying of success: if it dies, it will not be for this reason, because it still has a long, long way to go. But to go along that way it has to give brave and appealing offers in a changing world: it has to anticipate the future world right from within, from its roots.

4. Interiority and mystery

The eastern religions are curiously beginning to make their presence felt in the west, though cultural differences might have been expected to stunt their

---

[11] J.I. González Faus, *La humanidad nueva*, Santander, Sal Terrae, 1984, 6th ed.

[12] J. Habermas, *Legitimationsprobleme im Spätkapitalismus*, Frankfurt, Suhrkamp, 1973; "Creer y Saber", in *El Futuro de la Naturaleza Humana. ¿Hacia una eugenesia liberal?*, Barcelona, Paidós, 2002, pp. 129-146.

growth. Multiculturalism is said to be a fact that casts doubt on the possibility of certain human beings being able to communicate and make themselves understood with others, because they have different cultural heritages, and yet eastern religions are thriving to some degree in European societies, perhaps through the desire for change, which is doubtlessly one of the most common motivations in human beings, but perhaps also due to deeper motivations. One of these could be the fact that some eastern religions attempt to meet a need which is not discussed in democratic doctrines or in the ethical bases of supposed technological progress: the need to go more deeply into internal life, the urgency of recovering that internal "oneself" from which it is possible to get a dialogue under way with others. For there is indeed no "I" without "you", but finally neither is there any "you" without "I", in this existence of ours so thoroughly obsessed with exteriority.

For us walking down the street means deafening noise, watching out for cars, two people strolling along together but each chatting on the cell phone to someone else who is not there instead of talking to each other; getting home to the letter box in the hall, with messages on the answer phone, e-mails in the in-tray; yet more, endless bureaucracy to get some elementary activity done simply to survive; dozing in front of the television, being drained of life rather than having the soul filled; "spiritual meetings" in which everyone talks and there is no space to go into oneself; giving up that silence so essential to live as a person, serene reflection, "keeping all these things, pondering them over in the heart"; accepting Saint Augustine's invitation to "not go outward; return within yourself. In the inward man dwells truth".

It is indeed essential for there to be a change of structures, for there to be a revolution in relations between human beings, but without profound personal and non-transferable conversion in the heart, there cannot be any lasting transformation of the world. It is important to go to the root, and the source of changes, or the soil in which they have their roots, is the interior of each person. It is a pressing matter to recover internal life, create lifestyles with plenty of room for reflection, prayer, contact with the Spirit, without which there is no life, impetus, vital force, authenticity or dynamism. It is urgent to create ways of living in which there is space for profound conversion of the heart, to receive a heart of flesh, instead of a heart of stone which an inhuman world is making both possible and real, and to gain access to this mystery which requires time and silence.

Nevertheless Christianity has left the search delving into internal life too far behind and has let its very core become political; it has believed that personal life is only made in dialogue and deliberation, without recovering the most profound *being oneself* constituting an essential part.

But it also seems to have *given mystery up to a large extent* through a genuine "calculation error", believing that mystery is not within the reach of all personal fortunes. A religion with no mystery and no interiority seems much more acceptable, much more "sellable" than one which demands performing acts of faith in what is not fully rational, but indeed reasonable, only that the future of religions also depends on their interior dimension and mysteric quality.[13]

Ultimately the Episcopal papers say no more than any UNESCO bureaucrat could say: we should respect human rights, protect the environment, avoid xenophobia and racism, respect the elderly and handicapped, from whom we could learn so much, and all that "superficial bureaucratic morality" that anyone can distinguish with little room for error, because it is seen, read, heard and almost felt in all orthodox thinking and speaking. A flat discourse, with no relief, rather like a straight line on an electroencephalogram, with no ups and downs, as a sign of a life that monotonously vanishes with no vital force.

Nothing new. Church authorities organise congresses and forums on human rights, peace and the environment, punctually following UNESCO calendars, and only dropping the bureaucratic diet-morality script to attack abortion and euthanasia and cast doubts on genetic engineering. Is this really the "essence" of Christianity, its "competitive advantage"? Is this what will incite "potential customers" to display any interest in the product?

Talking of the good news in business terms will naturally smack of profanity to many ears and it is nevertheless not. The goods of the earth are social goods, and whoever believes he has the good of the good news to offer, because this really is happiness-making, whoever *really* believes this, will have to know why it can interest people who are tired of hearing these discourses and tired too of knowing that hardly anyone believes them and even fewer make them part of their everyday life. What can be offered today by a religion such as Christianity, to make people's heads turn and be of interest to someone who has not heard the message as something natural in the family, the school, the parish and the neighbourhood? What can make someone take this up as a way of living?

The formula is indeed simple: by recovering its core in a changing world. This means *demanding justice and doing it*, on the large scale but also on the small one, working side by side with the values of a *civic ethics* with which it feels at home, *offering and giving away grace*, beyond law and demandable duty, *recovering interiority*, without which there is no "I" from which to enter into a covenant with others, and not *giving up mystery,* to which we are vitally bonded. Interiority and mystery are two dimensions of human life that cannot be done away with, not only accessible to all rational and feeling beings, but only disdainfully rejected by the arrogant, intriguers and those who live out their lives prostrated to exteriority.

---

[13] P. Boyer, *The Naturalness of Religious Ideas. A Cognitive Theory of Religion*, Berkeley, University of California Press, 1994.

5. Going on telling other parables

All dimensions of culture are nourished on traditions and history and whoever knows beautiful narrations which make life fuller should go on recounting them, because the goods of the earth are social goods, and cannot be kept for oneself.

We started this book with two parables — that of *Genesis* and that of *Leviathan* — which have been passed down in different ways over recent centuries. This is why it is important to convey the silenced one, like many others that have been pushed out of the limelight. If history and traditions cease to be transmitted, someone who has never heard them will never be able to reconstruct them, just as no-one can reconstruct the history of a country if no-one has been told it. Traditions have to be told, and properly told, lived, and properly lived, to be the response to human beings' needs.

There do indeed continue to be a great deal of questions unanswered for us all, but what prevail are the values of a feeble pragmatism which would seem to make it difficult for religions to survive, but also for a civic ethics like the one we have mentioned above, and for a democratic politics which wishes to take justice seriously, as its task should be.

Because, as Nietzsche said, this democratic ethics which we defend with such conviction blooms in the shadow of the Jewish and Christian God who, in spite of all the distortions made by those who had the power to make them, mysteriously combines his face with the face of the other, links his holy destiny to the holy destiny of men, and women. For not in vain is Levinas, the philosopher of the "other's face", a Jew.

That is the reason why it is such a bad idea to give up those narrations which have gradually come to represent the best of the human being. That is why it even amounts to fraud to cease to tell them.

These stories, which in their deeper sense have been and still are a source of solidarity and peace, must on the contrary continue to be told. Dialogue must be fostered between religions to head into those dimensions of interiority and commitment, serenity and dedication, which make them a social good, and not a weapon.

PRINTED ON PERMANENT PAPER • IMPRIME SUR PAPIER PERMANENT • GEDRUKT OP DUURZAAM PAPIER - ISO 9706

N.V. PEETERS S.A., WAROTSTRAAT 50, B-3020 HERENT